The Quest for Progress

The Way We Lived in North Carolina, 1870–1920

© 1983 The University of North
Carolina Press

Manufactured in the United States
of America

*Library of Congress Cataloging in
Publication Data*

Nathans, Sydney.
    The quest for progress.

    Bibliography: p.
    1. North Carolina—History—1865–
2. North Carolina—Social life and
customs.   3. Historic sites—North
Carolina—Guide-books.   4. North
Carolina—Description and travel—
1981– —Guide-books. I. North
Carolina. Dept. of Cultural Resources.
II. Title.
F259.N4 1983   975.6′041   82-20133
ISBN 0-8078-1552-7
ISBN 0-8078-4104-8 (pbk.)

The Quest for Progress

The Way We Lived in North Carolina, 1870–1920

Published for the North Carolina Department of Cultural Resources

by The University of North Carolina Press   *Chapel Hill*

Editor:
Sydney Nathans

Consultants:
Larry Misenheimer
William S. Price, Jr.

This publication has been made possible through a grant from the National Endowment for the Humanities.

The Way We Lived series was developed under the guidance of the Historic Sites Section, Division of Archives and History, North Carolina Department of Cultural Resources.

(Title page) Farmers near the coast often used windmills like this one, no longer standing, at Beaufort, Carteret County, before commercial companies brought power to every farm. N.C. State Archives.

(Right) The transition from horse power to machine power can be seen in this view of Fayetteville St., Raleigh, about 1915. N.C. State Archives.

Christine Alexander took the photographs not otherwise credited.

Text by Sydney Nathans

Research and Marginalia by Jean B. Anderson

Design and Art Editing by Christine Alexander

Experiencing History

This series of books, *The Way We Lived*, is based on the premise that the past can be most fully comprehended through the combined impact of two experiences: reading history and visiting historic places. The text of this volume (the fourth in a series of five) is therefore coordinated with a variety of historical sites. Most places pictured as well as those mentioned in the margins are open to the public regularly or by appointment. Information about visiting and exact locations may be obtained locally.

Our objective in specifying sites has not been to compile a complete or comprehensive catalogue of historic places in the state; rather it has been to guide the reader to a representative selection of sites that exemplify the major themes of the text.

Many excellent examples that might have served our purpose equally well have been omitted. Others now in the planning or working stages of restoration may be expected to swell the number of unnamed sites. We can only leave to the readers the pleasure of their discovery and the hope that this volume will serve as a stimulus to further reading and exploration.

Contents

Aberdeen and Rockfish Railroad, 1898.
N.C. State Archives.

Overview

The Industrial Age

Americans by 1870 had grown accustomed to the notion that boundaries were made to be broken. In the previous half-century, the United States had become a continental nation, begun its ascent as the manufacturing titan of the globe, overcome the distances between its cities and its shores with fifty thousand miles of railroad tracks, and emancipated the enslaved members of its society after a four-year Civil War.

Yet, even for those who took for granted that change was an American way of life, the transformations of the next fifty years came on a scale and with a completeness that proved startling. New inventions hastened the pace of life and work for millions. Electric power and the electric trolley, the telephone and the typewriter, the automobile and the airplane, made acceleration synonymous with American society. The physical scale of virtually everything exploded. In business, Standard Oil, the American Tobacco Company, and United States Steel were but a few of the giant industries that emerged by the turn of the century—their work forces in the thousands, their capital in the hundreds of millions, their power and influence unparalleled. In the half-century after 1870, the nation's population doubled from fifty to a hundred million. Americans from the countryside and immigrants from abroad swarmed to the nation's cities and gave the United States an urban majority by 1920. One of every ten Americans lived in a city of more than a million. The surging growth of cities and the expansion of the nation's railway network to two hundred thousand miles set the stage for mass production, mass advertising, and accumulation of vast fortunes. If Andrew Jackson and Abraham Lincoln stood as symbols of the self-made men of the nineteenth century, Andrew Carnegie and Henry Ford—the one a corporate empire-builder, the other the master of assembly-line production—embodied values of the twentieth.

The new possibilities of American life created new pressures. Cities with skyscrapers and clanging trolleys and diverse inhabitants, though exhilarating to many, proved unsettling to others. Many people placed a new premium on privacy and sought refuge from the raucousness of life in enlarged homes or suburban neighborhoods, in exclusive clubs or remote resorts. The growing intensity of work led to a new emphasis on the need for relaxation. Baseball became a national pastime, bicycling became a craze, and Coney Island and

Arrival of first streetcar, Goldsboro, Wayne County, ca. 1908. N.C. State Archives.

When Captain William J. Tate answered Orville and Wilbur Wright's inquiry about Kitty Hawk as a site for their glider experiments, he won for North Carolina a role in their historic victory. "If you decide to try your machine & come I will take pleasure in doing all I can for your convenience & success & pleasure, & I assure you you will find a hospitable people when you come among us." Kelly, ed., *Miracle at Kitty Hawk*.

The Wright Brothers National Memorial, Kitty Hawk, Dare County, chronicles the history of their struggle to fly and the moment on 17 December 1903 when their heavier-than-air, power-driven machine rose in the face of a twenty-seven-mile-per-hour wind and changed the course of human events.

other amusement parks flourished as places of release and revelry away from the cares of the job.

In the half-century after the Civil War, a new industrial society emerged in the United States and renewed the country's historic promise as a land of opportunity. Yet, though the nation was one of new invention, new wealth, and new diversions, a gnawing question loomed large. Who would reap the gains of the immensely productive and powerful society that emerged by the end of the nineteenth century? Farmers wondered as they saw their bumper crops turn into harvests of debt and dependency in the 1880s and 1890s. Factory workers wondered as they found themselves forced to subordinate their ingenuity and work habits to the demands of machinery and intensified supervision. Enterprising businessmen wondered as they confronted corporations of enormous size and power. Black Americans and ambitious women, their hopes stirred by the expansive energies of the nation, wondered whether or not the country's new opportunities included them. The answer for all was clear by the turn of the century. Gains would not come without struggle. The age of unprecedented riches produced a generation of rebels.

The Tar Heel State

Though North Carolina had been spared the worst ravages of the Civil War, few would have predicted in 1870 that the "Rip van Winkle" state would within fifty years become the most industrialized state in the South. Communities that were still barely hamlets five years after the war's end, such as Durham and Winston, and towns that served as commercial centers for surrounding countryside, such as Greensboro and Charlotte, would in the decades ahead become centers of industry. But factories did not burgeon in cities alone. A rushing stream and a willing work force opened the way for the creation of mill villages in the countryside wherever the capital could be collected. The value of goods manufactured in North Carolina was less than ten million dollars in 1870. It was almost a billion by 1920.

Though the folkways of country life persisted into the twentieth century, rural North Carolina was also transformed. Emancipation set the stage for the emergence of tenancy and sharecropping as the predominant labor system for the black farmers of the state. The coming of the railroads and the growth of commercial centers opened the way for thousands of white and black farmers to shift from subsistence agriculture to a concentration on the growth of cash crops. Greatest was the expansion of the tobacco crop of the state, which by the turn of the century surpassed a hundred million pounds. By 1920 North Carolina tobacco filled many of the nation's cigarettes and pipes.

Princeville, Edgecombe County. Photograph by Walton Haywood. N.C. State Archives. Freed slaves started the community as Freedom Hill in 1865. When the town was incorporated in 1885, the name was changed to honor a resident, Turner Prince.

For black North Carolinians, the half-century after 1870 was a time of new freedom, new striving, and new setbacks. Enfranchised through federal law by the 1870s and politically active for three decades thereafter, they saw their voting and civil rights systematically revoked by state legislation after 1900. Widely employed as skilled artisans in North Carolina towns through the 1890s, they found their opportunities increasingly restricted and confined after the turn of the century. Throughout the uncertain years between legal emancipation and legal segregation and amidst the adversity intensified by disfranchisement and formal passage of Jim Crow laws, blacks built communities, churches, colleges, and business enterprises. The black institutions fashioned between 1870 and 1920 nurtured the spiritual strength and commitment to racial betterment that ultimately provided powerful resources for a renewed struggle to reclaim their rights.

Finally, in this half-century, the rustic beauty of North Carolina, long familiar to inhabitants, was discovered by other Americans. The western part of the state, with its fresh air and relaxed pace, became a haven of health for the ill. By the 1890s travelers seeking recuperation and relaxation away from the congested Northeast found in the breathtaking mountains of the west and the sandhills of the Coastal Plain an ideal place to play. North Carolina became the site of a boom for recreation of all sorts.

A Nash County farm, ca. 1910. N.C.
State Archives. Tobacco culture involved
everyone: black and white, men and
women, young and old.

The Rural World

In 1920, for the first time in American history, the United States census revealed that a majority of Americans lived in urban areas. Not so in North Carolina. Despite the steady growth of towns and cities and the dramatic expansion of industry in the state, in the fifty years after 1870 the lives of most North Carolinians remained rooted in agriculture and centered on the farm.

Between city and countryside the contrasts intensified. Machinery and a ceaseless flood of inventions accelerated the pace and expanded the scale of city life: electric power, the telephone, the typewriter, steel for skyscrapers, the automobile, moving pictures, the wireless radio. The latest wonders of technology found their way to some Tar Heel farms, to be sure. Yet the predominant rhythm of life remained rural; the hoe and the plow persisted as the essential tools for work, and the power supply of the farm continued to be men and mules—"machines with meat." Above all, between metropolis and hinterland there emerged a growing contrast in wealth. Despite appalling urban poverty, the cities' upper class grew rich as never before, and all city folk seemed devoted to making money. Until the turn of the twentieth century, notwithstanding moments and scattered examples of prosperity, most North Carolina farmers were locked in a struggle to subsist. For many it remained an achievement to "make do."

Spring plowing on a mountain farm. Photograph by Margaret Morley (1858–1923). N.C. State Archives. This, like many pictures to follow, is among Morley's rich collection of photographs taken near Tryon, Polk County, during her summer vacations in the early years of this century. She is better known, however, for her nature study books for children.

Making Do

Day by day, season by season, agricultural life in the state after 1870 seemed to perpetuate much that was unchanged from the past. The major crops were those that had predominated before the Civil War—tobacco, cotton, corn—and the methods of work were little altered. Tobacco had to be tended constantly by hand. When the tobacco was ready for harvest, women and children brought the ripe leaves to the tobacco shed, and men hung them to age and cure. Young and old alike knew and executed the mysteries of curing—tending the fire that slowly drew the excess moisture from the leaves, telling tales through the aromatic nights, and, when the tobacco was ready, taking the crop to market for its sale. Cotton made similar demands on the hand labor of the entire family. After plowing and planting, the primary task was "chopping"—not the cotton plant but the hungry weeds that competed relentlessly for the nutrients of the soil.

". . . frontier customs, based on neighborliness, charity, and necessity, survived in log rollings, house raisings, corn shuckings, hog killings, and quilting." Taylor, *Carolina Crossroads*.

5

Fruit could be preserved if it was dried. Apples drying in a mountain cabin. Photograph by Margaret Morley. N.C. State Archives.

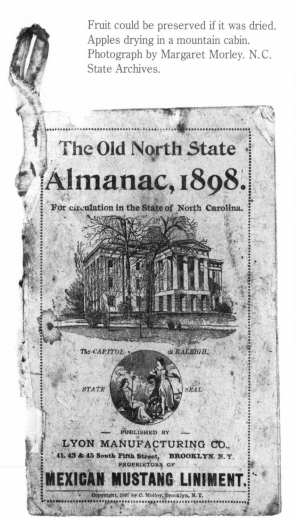

James King Wilkerson Papers. "Almanacs, distributed free by makers of patent medicines, were suspended from a nail just underneath the fireplace mantel for consultation concerning the weather, phases of the moon, and factual information which was interspersed with testimonials of miraculous cures of this-or-that ailment through the faithful use of the advertised product." Taylor, *Carolina Crossroads.*

When home remedies failed, the doctor was consulted. Two doctors' offices, of 1857 and 1890, are combined and restored in the Country Doctor Museum, Bailey, Nash County. One part displays the apothecary and library of a doctor; the other, an office and medical instruments.

As in the past, so in the late nineteenth century, the calendar of the crops dictated the activities of the year: plowing, planting, harvesting; corn shucking, tobacco curing, cotton ginning. Such were the seasonal demarcations of life. There were special times for relaxation and fun: long country nights filled with stories spun before the fireplace; summer circuses on Saturday afternoons; weekend "frolics" at "different houses the country round," when hosts would clear out a room and invite neighbors to "kick up and dance" to the music of accordians and fiddles, banjos, and washboards. But often recreation dovetailed with work. Improvised field "hollers," sung at a high-pitched shout, relieved the solitude of a man working alone in the field. Hot suppers followed community work-gatherings such as a barn raising or a corn shucking. The county fair mixed whiskey and whimsy with the pageant of products from the farm.

Familiar ways of farming, year-round family labor, and seasonal celebrations persisted in North Carolina well into the twentieth century. That way of life is visible today in the Great Smoky Mountains of Appalachia at the Pioneer Farmstead of Swain County. Until the early decades of this century, the same way of life could have been observed flourishing in neighborhoods of the Blue Ridge or far to the east in the tenant houses and sharecropper cabins of black freedmen, first-generation pioneers in the enterprise of small-scale agriculture and family self-sufficiency.

Of course, there were important differences between the white settlers of the west, the landowning yeomen throughout the state who had farmed independently for generations, and the postwar black and white tenants of the Piedmont and Coastal Plain. Most newly emancipated blacks began their lives as freedmen in cramped "slavery-time cabins." Made of logs, with one room down and one room up, the typical home had a few small window openings, wooden shutters to close off the cabin from the elements, and an earthen floor that was "hard as cement." Most had log chimneys plastered with mud and stone. A barrel of water rested nearby to douse a fire if it got out of control, and a ladder stood handy to topple an inflamed

At the Pioneer Farmstead, U.S. #441, Great Smoky Mountains National Park, Swain County, daily chores and methods of a vanished past are demonstrated. Well water in a dish is a primitive sink; a cloth over the food and a paper fly-swatter on the wall do the job of window screens.

chimney away from the cabin. Only over time, as some tenants became landowners and others became long-term sharecroppers for the same owner, did the physical appearance of the homestead become less rudimentary. Gradually, the sharecropper's house might change with the addition of larger windows paned with glass, board-and-batten siding to cover the log exterior, and perhaps even a small shed porch to keep the rain from beating through the front door.

Far outweighing differences between rural tenants and landowners, however, was a common necessity that bound thousands of North Carolina farm families into a shared pattern of life. All had to be resourceful to survive. Visitors to the Pioneer Homestead can see rural resourcefulness on display and in practice in the farm cabin, sorghum mill, blacksmith shed, and bee-gum stand. Demonstrators —both male and female—show the skills and folk knowledge that passed from one generation to the next. The ingenuity, the patience, and the pride of those who "made do"—and did without—surprise and delight the guest.

At the root of dozens of shared customs was shared scarcity. East and west in rural North Carolina, those who "come up poor" were the majority. Rural ingenuity enabled thousands of farming families to live on their own resources with little cash income. "Making do" involved the women of a household in the production of their own soap by boiling lye and animal fat. It meant plucking geese or chickens to make downy feather beds for the grown-ups, stuffing corn shucks or straw into bed-ticks for the young. "Getting by" meant a large garden and as much cropland as could be spared given over to raising one's own food: corn, wheat, sweet potatoes, orchards, milk cows, hogs, goats. And it meant knowing how to salt the meat and preserve the fruit and vegetables. "Making do" meant feed-sack blankets to keep in the warmth on snowy nights, quilts crafted from colorful scraps of cloth, rugs woven of bright yarn. It meant clothing sewn at home—and then patching and more patching, so "it got to where we couldn't tell where the clothes left off and the patches began." It meant a knowledge of folk medicine: how to use snake oil to lubricate childbirth and how large a dose of calomel to give the grandchildren each spring "to cleanse them out," as well as how much was healthy

Mingus Mill, Pioneer Farmstead. Other working mills from the period are Jessup's Mill, S.R. #1432 north of Francisco, Stokes County, built ca. 1903, and Laurel Mill, S.R. #1432, Gupton vicinity, northeast of Louisburg, Franklin County, which may incorporate an antebellum mill.

A felled tree served as a footbridge. Photograph by Margaret Morley. N.C. State Archives.

Country churches surviving from this period are numerous. Following are some examples: Chapel of the Good Shepherd, 1871, Ridgeway vicinity, Warren County; Piney Creek Primitive Baptist Church, 1875, Alleghany County; Grassy Creek Methodist Church, 1904, Ashe County; and Lystra Baptist Church, 1852, Lystra Church Rd. off U.S. #15-501, Chatham County.

and how much would "take your teeth out." It meant relying on community midwives or "granny women" to deliver babies.

Whether they owned their land or worked someone else's, North Carolina farm families rarely relied on their own resources alone. Sharing was a vital feature of country living. While the crops were growing, a family "caught up" on its work might help neighbors and relatives with theirs. In times of need—illness, death, accident, debt—family members contributed food and support to each other. Many of the young continued to choose their mates among close neighbors and to reside in home communities that abounded with cousins and kin. Family ties and well-worn footpaths known to those in the community provided links and grassy highways from home to home. Sundays would see the members of each community gather at a neighborhood church in their Sabbath best. Whatever the denomination, whatever the race, most rural religion was communal and fervid. Sunday brought the sharing of fellowship, release, and spiritual renewal.

The Perils of Productivity

Continuities of custom there were, yet in dramatic and paradoxical ways rural life in North Carolina was transformed by 1890.

To begin with, the plantation system was gone, ended by the Civil War and emancipation. Had the former masters had their way, black freedmen would have stayed on the old home-place and continued to work under strict supervision in exchange for food, housing, and a nominal wage. Most blacks rejected such terms, so similar to slavery. But, because emancipation brought freedmen neither land nor mules, seed nor credit, most settled for the halfway houses of tenancy or sharecropping and farmed a portion of a white owner's land as renters or for a third to a half-share of the crop. For former planters, the new system provided at least laborers for their land, though profits fell. For the black sharecroppers or tenants, the new order afforded a limited but vital measure of freedom—the freedom to live well away from the "Big House," to decide whether the wife and the children of the family would work and at what pace they would labor, to choose what goods they would buy with their livelihood, and perhaps above all the right to serve the Lord in their own church and to seek an education for themselves and their children.

Yet by the 1880s it was clear that a second change—as momentous as emancipation—was under way in rural North Carolina. Thousands of the state's farmers began growing the bulk of their crops for market. The shift seemed eminently sensible. The reconstruction of the state's railroads, the growth of towns and industries, and the multiplication of cotton gins and tobacco warehouses, where crops

10

could be hauled in a day and sold for cash on the spot, made it entirely practical to farm for profit. With a little credit for mules and tools, with a small advance that would cover the cost of food and goods no longer produced at home, cultivators had every reason to hope that the days of postwar poverty were behind them and that they could get ahead at last.

In case Piedmont farmers had their doubts about concentrating on the cash crop, the brash boosters of rapidly multiplying tobacco warehouses labored to allay their fears. In Goldsboro and Rocky Mount, in Winston and Durham, in Kinston and Oxford, and in dozens of other towns of the state the warehouses still come to life in mid-August and brim with bright leaf tobacco until October. Warehouse transactions are businesslike and routine now, but in the 1870s and for decades thereafter they were sights and sounds to behold.

Feverish competition for the farmer's tobacco crop began in the countryside with the mid-summer appearance everywhere of auctioneers' broadsides promising high profits and a "down-home" welcome. Posters and boldly painted signs, the billboards of their day, brightened the exteriors of hundreds of barns and signaled that market time was near. Once the farmer loaded his sturdy Nissen wagon —canvas-covered to protect the crop, ruggedly designed to navigate the crudest roads—he journeyed to town and unloaded his leaves and himself in the warehouse, where both often spent the night. The next morning, in a cavernous building festooned with flags on the outside and full of bustle and shouting within, he loosely piled up his leaves for the buyers to eye and appraise. Then the auctioneer went to it, "crying the bids like lightning and never a drop of sweat in his collar." Jovial and exuberant, he rarely missed a telltale wink or nod, salute or out-stuck tongue, among the herd of bidders. In 1870 an auctioneer could dispatch a pile of leaves a minute; by 1920 he closed a sale every nine seconds. The farmer had his cash in hand ten minutes after the final bid. Then came time to relax, to enjoy the medicine show and banjo-picking outside the warehouse, to wend his way through the peddlers hawking their wares, and perhaps to wander uptown to stores that gladly received him. Throngs came to watch the show, which gave profit and pleasure to all.

No less than the city warehouse, the country store seemed a godsend to the farmer eager for a chance to make money and to acquire store-bought goods. The merchant furnished plow-points, fertilizer, and seed, all essential for farming. He sold cornmeal, molasses, and hog meat, the Three Ms that were basic staples for many, and carried as well an abundant supply of link sausages and pepper-seasoned sardines. Corsets, fine calicoes, and nursing nipples, copper-toed shoes and shaving razors—all could be found on the merchant's shelves. And, like the tobacco warehouse, the country store provided more than goods. It offered a congenial setting for

Pepper's warehouse, ca. 1919, Winston-Salem, Forsyth County, and Fenner's warehouse, Rocky Mount, Edgecombe County, are typical specimens of the period.

Cotton going to market, 1898. Tompkins, *History of Mecklenburg County*, vol. 1.

"We'd leave home one morning, spend the night on the road, and get into Durham the next afternoon. We'd take our tobacco to Cap'n Parrish's place; he had a warehouse on what's now Parrish Street. . . . When we'd get close to town he'd have a pair of big mules waiting to hitch on and haul us in to the warehouse. The mud in the streets sometimes would be knee-deep to a mule. He had stalls for the horses and mules and quarters for farmers, some would sleep in their wagons. Everybody brought their victuals. Now as soon as a farmer gets to town he hits out for a café. Every warehouse has to have one to take care of him." Clyde Singleton's memories in Banks, ed., *First-Person America.*

Swindell's store, Bath, Beaufort County. Many store buildings from the period remain: File's general store, Bringle Ferry Rd. near Morgan, Rowan County; the store at Hamer, Caswell County; Lacy's store, Bahama, Durham County; O. O. Rufty's general store, Salisbury, Rowan County; and the Mast store, Valle Crucis, Watauga County. Few, however, maintain their old character and general merchandise.

country people to gather, swap stories, play checkers, and more than occasionally put away a little whiskey. One rarely had to travel far to find this cornucopia. A country merchant was usually no more than ten or twelve miles from most of his customers.

But the most important commodity provided by the "furnishing merchant" to farmers was not found on his shelves, but in his ledger books. That commodity was credit. With so few banks and so little money in the postwar South—there was one bank for every fifty-eight thousand southerners in 1895, one for every sixteen thousand inhabitants outside the region—the merchant who advanced supplies without cash was a makeshift banker and a welcome one.

Access to railroads and warehouses, merchants and credit—to many these developments heralded the birth of a New South in agriculture. Writing in 1881, Atlanta journalist and promoter Henry Grady celebrated the emergence of a "prosperous self-respecting race of small farmers, cultivating their own lands, living upon their own resources, controlling their crops until they are sold, and independent alike of usurers and provision brokers." The view of the South as an emerging patchwork of "small farmers" found support in the official returns of the United States census from 1860 to 1900. In those four decades, the number of small farms in North Carolina tripled from 75,000 to 225,000, while the average size of landholdings fell by two-thirds, from an average of 316 acres to 101. The patterns revealed for North Carolina were similar throughout the South.

Unfortunately, the agricultural statistics of the census were utterly misleading, as perhaps any observant traveler through the state would have detected. The census categorized tenants and share-croppers as "small farmers," and hence its numbers masked the steady rise of economic dependency among whites and blacks. Even landowning farmers who were self-sufficient found themselves in jeopardy. Far from an agrarian paradise of independent yeomen, the North Carolina that emerged in the 1880s found itself gradually entrapped in new forms of servitude. Lured and then addicted to the production of cash crops, the state's farmers married their fortunes to the marketplace at a time when prices for farm products were about to collapse all over the globe.

Farmers went into debt to prepare and fertilize their crops and to provision their families during the year. Devoting most of their land and time to cash crops, they purchased food they had once raised for themselves and ready-made merchandise they had once fashioned on the farm. At the year's end, time and again, they discovered that the very abundance of the harvest had depressed agricultural prices. The cost of credit and warehousing and transport became crucial in making the difference between profit and loss—yet these costs were high and seemingly beyond the farmers' control. Nor was there any easy escape back to subsistence. Under the crop-

The unending struggle of the poor just to exist, usually housed in cold, cheerless, bug-ridden cabins, took its toll as the faces of this family show. Photograph by Margaret Morley. N.C. State Archives.

"And everybody in the country had chinches [bedbugs]. I'd just hate that so bad—'bout twice a year we had to carry everything out of the house, and Mother would fill our big old wash pot full of water and get it hot and then she'd go in there and throw it all over the walls and scald all the walls down good. And it wasn't just us that did that; it was everybody." Ginns, *Rough Weather Makes Good Timber.*

lien system, when the farmer did not "pay out" his debt to the landlord or furnishing merchant, he was legally bound to give the creditor a mortgage on his next year's crop. So he labored to produce still more tobacco and more cotton. Yet greater production seemed to bring only lower prices and profits. By 1890 one of three white farmers and three of four black farmers in the state found themselves tenants or sharecroppers—and the rest were fearful. The unintended harvest of the plunge into commercial agriculture was an annual bonanza crop of debt and dependency.

THE PHOTOGRAPH, THE REEL AND THE GIRL, ALL NORTH CAROLINA PRODUCTS.

D. A. TOMPKINS COMPANY,
MANUFACTURERS,
CHARLOTTE, N. C.

D. A. Tompkins Company, cotton manufacturers in Charlotte, Mecklenburg County, put the best face on working conditions in this illustration. N.C. State Archives. Farm women and girls were attracted to factory jobs despite long hours and tiring work because they could be sure of steady wages and relief from the isolation and muck of farm life.

Zelma Murray described the spinning room she worked in as "awful linty," and Ethel Faucette looked back happily to her first factory job: "I made eighty-five cents a day." Southern Oral History Program (SOHP), University of North Carolina.

Reform and Revolt

By the mid-1880s it was becoming evident to many a farming family that the production of crops for market was not the road to independence. Farm owners and tenants alike knew by the eighties that something needed to be done, but what? As it turned out, three courses of action opened up to rural North Carolinians.

One possibility was simply to leave the countryside altogether. Departure depended in part on opportunity. As the towns of the Piedmont grew and became places where the ambitious might hope to get ahead and where the curious might hope to sample the life of the larger world, young people left in search of urban advantages. But most of those who deserted the farm did so because they had no choice. Young, single individuals streamed to such burgeoning towns as Greenville, Durham, Charlotte, and Asheville. Blacks took on day labor, domestic work, or jobs in the stemmeries of tobacco factories, while whites found jobs tending textile and tobacco machinery. As agricultural depression intensified in the 1890s, the ranks of migrants swelled and became dominated by entire families, who packed up possessions on mule-drawn wagons and said farewell to the land.

But, though thousands of North Carolinians left the land, even more remained. Both the number of farms and farmers continued to grow through the 1930s. First for a handful, then for an ever-increasing number of the rural majority, a second path emerged as the means of deliverance from the tangle of debt and dependency. Eventually called "scientific agriculture," and today magnified in the agribusiness mega-farms that fertilize the soil with chemicals and reap crops and profits with machines, the technological highway to salvation had its bedrock base in the 1880s. "Improvement" and better management would make the progressive farmer free.

The campus of North Carolina State University today is a sprawling monument to the message of better farms through better management and to the ultimate surrender of mules and tradition to machines and technical know-how. The university would bring delight to the eyes of those who in the 1880s had crusaded for its birth. Initially a handful of journalists and legislative leaders, they were mostly men born on small farms who had come to know a wider world when they traveled away to college or war or moved to town in the wake of the Confederacy's defeat. In the decade of the eighties, their target was modernizing the agriculture (and the industry) of their native state—with a land-grant college as the trailblazer of reform.

Undisputed voice of the crusaders was Leonidas L. Polk, founder in 1886 of the newspaper the *Progressive Farmer*. A man of Franklinian curiosity and enterprise, Polk had a vitality that found its way into dozens of undertakings. Born to an Anson County small planter in 1837, Polk during the next half-century was a farmer, state legislator (at the age of twenty-three), Confederate soldier, town developer, storekeeper, patent-medicine inventor, and in 1877 the state's first commissioner of agriculture. But he saw the newspaper he began in the mid-1880s as "my chosen lifework" and viewed his mission as persuading North Carolinians to fight rural impoverishment by substituting "solid, demonstrated *facts*" for hidebound farming habits. Whether it was a "remedy for the staggers in hogs" or "Why Daughters Should Be Taught Housework," the Raleigh editor urged farmers to seek and exchange information and to try new ideas. With nearly eleven thousand subscribers in 1890, the *Progressive Farmer* had the largest circulation of any newspaper in the state. When politicians dragged their feet over the creation of an agricultural college, Polk mounted a yearlong editorial campaign that was relentless, blistering, and—in 1887—triumphant.

Polk and the other advocates of progressive farm management had high hopes for the work to go on in the agricultural college's first building, Holladay Hall. Today housing the administration that presides over thousands of students and dozens of buildings, the Richardsonian Romanesque structure was erected in 1888 and later named after the school's first president. The reformers of the eighties watched with satisfaction as the first young men came from their farms to learn from agricultural experts and laboratories the latest techniques that research had revealed. Young women followed in the 1890s. They discovered in the classrooms that homemaking and nutrition were no less matters for rational management and learned that the savings from home canning could purchase the comforts of an indoor commode. But the college did not simply wait passively for learners to come to Raleigh for baptism in the ways of progress. After 1900 a second generation of reformers took their message to the field through the state Agricultural Extension Service, founded in 1906, and through the county agent program. The progressives' campaign to improve soil and homes, to eradicate insects and ignorance, to encourage "Two-Armed Farming"—a balance of crops and livestock—was in full swing by 1910.

But, as Alliance Hall in Columbus County reminds us, by no means did all North Carolina farmers deal with the problem of agricultural depression through the remedies of migration or improved management. For those who joined the Farmers' Alliance in the 1880s and who met for over a decade at this now silent and solitary hall, the best way for farmers to defend themselves was to band together—and fight.

Those who conducted meetings in Alliance Hall, who questioned speakers and debated choices, were angry. They were among a hundred thousand North Carolinians and three million nationally who joined a massive farmers' movement to combat the stranglehold of sinking prices and high costs. Whatever the crop, the story was

Holladay Hall, Raleigh, Wake County. North Carolina State University's first building, 1888, was made of brick fired by prisoners. N.C. Collection, Louis R. Wilson Library, University of North Carolina.

In the 1870s an industrialist of Gaston County saw the farmer's individualism as his obstacle to prosperity: "Prejudice is allways a formidable barier to truth and the farmers unfounded dread and hostility to coopiration and acting together for their common good stands more in his way to wealth and usefulness than the want of capital and all other causes besides." Stowe Family Papers.

Alliance Hall, U.S. #701 north of Whiteville, Columbus County. Courtesy Thom Billington, photographer.

everywhere the same in the bleak eighties: "five-cent cotton, ten-cent meat." Credit charges on advances of food and supplies from furnishing merchants ran from 40 to 60 percent. Interest on bank loans, freight charges by railroads, fees for warehousemen—each expense seemed increasingly exorbitant and unaffordable, and the sum of the debts murderous. Thousands of tenants, obliged by liens on their crops to plant all their acreage in a money crop and to buy the bulk of their needs at the creditors' stores, were in virtual peonage. Thousands of landowners feared the loss of their farms and descent into "tenantry and peasantry." They were in desperate straits.

The Farmers' Alliance movement that swept out of Texas in the late 1880s offered a powerful democratic answer to despair: cooperation. Consumer and producer cooperatives, organized and run by the farmers themselves, would drastically cut the cost of the middleman, would reduce credit charges from a crushing 60 percent to 2, and would allow farmers to hold crops at their own cooperative warehouses until the market price was right. Here was a chance for battered men and women who had come to look on themselves as destined only for annual economic defeat to regain control of their futures. As one Allianceman wrote, "we are going to get out of debt and be free and independent people once more."

When Alliance speakers brought the call for economic cooperation to North Carolina in 1887, the results were spectacular. The state Alliance leader reported that twenty-one North Carolina organizers were not enough. He needed a hundred. In one county there was not "an interval of five miles" that did not have an Alliance chapter. "The farmers seem like unto ripe fruit. You can gather them by the gentle shake of a bush." At the year's end he reported that there were eleven hundred suballiances and forty thousand members. By 1890 membership stood at ninety thousand and cooperatives were flourishing. Members could take their tobacco to Alliance warehouses in Oxford and Durham. They could buy a wide array of goods from the Alliance "State Business Agency" at Hillsborough, each item offered "at wholesale prices." Seeds, fertilizers, buggies, cook stoves, corn shellers, pianos, washing machines, guns, "Loaded Shells, etc. etc."—all were sold with the "middle man's profit" going to the farmer. As a means to family self-sufficiency, the Alliance's state agency particularly recommended the "Improved High Arm Alliance Sewing Machine"—"Our Price, $18.50, Agents Ask for $45.00"—which had "gone into all classes of homes, rich and poor," and which fearlessly "withstood the unskilled use of those formerly unaccustomed to Sewing Machines." By the early 1890s North Carolinians had Alliance tanneries, sawmills, even shoe factories. Cooperation extended to charity as well as to consumer goods, as in the case of the Alliance chapter that raised $180 to replace the horse of a "poor man with an invalid wife and six small children."

Yet something more fundamental was to occur in the Alliance halls of North Carolina and of the South than the creation of charity associations and Alliance discount stores. Members soon found themselves clashing head-on with bankers and merchants, railroads and warehousemen, none eager to sacrifice their profits to the cooperative competitors. When cooperatives and farmers' exchanges sought credit, they found it scarce and costly. But the problem was more than local or even statewide. Credit and the currency supply of the entire nation, it became evident, were in the viselike grip of the country's largest private bankers, who in the name of "sound currency" had dictated two decades of deflation and tight money. By 1890 the Farmers' Alliance was well on its way toward becoming an insurgent political party, compelled and prepared to take on the vast private interests—bankers, railroads—that held them in thrall and to challenge the two major parties, which seemed indifferent to their plight.

Scientific agriculture and agricultural protest were not exclusive but complementary strategies for reform. No life better illustrates their connection—and the forces that drove reformers into insurgency—than the career of Leonidas L. Polk. In 1887 the editor of the *Progressive Farmer* became head of the North Carolina Alliance. He proved as magnetic in the meeting hall as he had been persuasive with the pen. "My own father was one of thousands," a North Carolinian recalled, "who thought of Col. Polk almost as if he had been a God-given Moses to lead them out of the wilderness." Elected president of the National Alliance in 1889, he crisscrossed the country for the next three years, urging farmers from Michigan to Georgia, Kansas to the Carolinas, to trample "sectionalism under our feet" and build a great coalition for the "coming struggle."

By 1892 Polk was a transformed man. The state agricultural reformer had become national leader of a mass democratic rebellion. In February of that year, speaking in St. Louis, he called for "the great West, the great South, and the great Northwest, to link their hands and hearts together and march to the ballot box and take possession of the government and run it in the interest of the people." He pressed for a revolution at the ballot box and was the certain presidential nominee in 1892 of the rebellious new People's party. The Populist demands of 1892 were no less than extraordinary: government control of the nation's banking system and currency, national ownership of the country's railroads, publicly owned warehouses to hold the crops of farmers, and government loans and credit at an interest rate of 1 percent a year. Only Polk's sudden death at the age of fifty-five three weeks before the convention denied him the Populist nomination. But by then the Alliance movement had evolved radically from the cooperative crusade. As farm wives and daughters dispensed lemonade outside of Alliance halls throughout North Caro-

Leonidas L. Polk (1837–92). N.C. State Archives.

In 1913 the *Progressive Farmer* employed a full-time women's editor who crusaded in her columns for rural clubs for the lonely, overburdened farm wives. She discussed health, food preparation, and home improvement, reinforcing the magazine's view that woman's place was in the home.

lina and the nation, speakers held forth under a banner reading "Down with monopoly for Labor is King."

Notwithstanding the death of their leader and division in Alliance ranks over participation in politics, the Populists of North Carolina did "march to the ballot box." Throughout the decade of the 1890s they constituted an immense force for innovation in the state. The Populist entry into politics shattered the complacent indifference of the state's Democratic party, brought the election of Populist-supported candidates for governor and United States senator, and radically transformed the legislature and the laws of the state. In the governor's race of 1892, the candidates of the state's Populist and Republican parties won a majority of the votes cast but failed to unite. In 1894 and 1896 the Populists fused their fortunes and electoral ticket with the Republicans, and the results were resounding victories for an unprecedented alliance that crossed party and racial lines.

Despite mutual misgivings, Populists and Republicans, white farmers and black, subordinated their suspicions to goals that they shared. The "Fusion" movement stood committed to elections open to all male voters and to balloting free of fraud—"a free vote and a fair count." The coalition stood for longer and better schooling for all the state's children, for the firm regulation of the state's railroads, for a legal interest rate of 6 percent, and for an end to the subservience of state government to business interests.

Triumph nonetheless set the stage for tragedy: a campaign of terror in 1898 that routed the coalition in the name of "White Supremacy." The hope proclaimed by the banner that bedecked the

Subscription schools continued after public schools were set up. Minnie Lee Spencer remembered hers well: "We used to go to subscription schools, and my pappy would pay for me. Seems like it was sometimes a dollar a month. . . . I remember it was just a little bit of a log cabin, and you could stick your fingers down through the cracks in the floor.

"There was one single row of windows by the workbench. That was all the light we had, don't you know. But they were all broken out and it was open through there. The bottom of the door was worn away, too. . . .

"We went just three months during the cold winter-time. We had a big old fire-place, and the teacher and children would go out to the woods and bring in brush to make a fire. Then there was a spring right near there. If we wanted a drink of water, we went to the spring. . . .

"We had six lessons a day: Blue Back spelling, arithmetic, reading. . . . Then we had history and geography, and . . . I can't remember what the other one was called. . . . Grammar? I guess that's what it was—grammar." Ginns, *Rough Weather Makes Good Timber.*

A mountain school, ca. 1900. N.C. State Archives.

The former Philadelphus community schoolhouse may be seen at the Robeson County Educational Resource Center, N.C. #72 northwest of Lumberton. Other one-room schoolhouses have been rescued and restored: one has been moved to Governor Aycock's Birthplace, Wayne County; another from the black community of Bellview is now located at the Moore County Board of Education grounds, U.S. #1 south of Sanford.

Alliance halls of 1892, "Down with Monopoly for Labor is King," was extinguished by force. The white robes used by Ku Klux Klan night riders in the 1860s gave way to the Red Shirts of new vigilantes in 1898, worn openly in the light of day. Despite the fact that whites never for a moment relinquished control of the Fusion alliance—only eight of the Republican governor's eight hundred appointees were black—the incessant cry of "Negro Domination" leaped from every Democratic newspaper and stump speech. Though over half the eligible black electorate risked their safety to vote, thousands who had voted in earlier elections stayed home. Populists defected in droves to the standard of racial self-preservation. Democrats won a smashing victory, and their triumph set the stage for Populist extinction, black disfranchisement, and the reign of Jim Crow.

Rising farm prices in the early twentieth century and particularly during World War I removed much of the urgency and desperation that had fueled the farmer's movement. Even in times of greater well-being, some farmers experimented with cooperatives and farmers' unions to control prices and credit. A more socially responsive Democratic party took up the Populist call for universal public education and railroad regulation, though Democratic educational expenditures in fact favored the school districts of the white and well-to-do, and though the regulatory commission worked compliantly with the railroads. Tranquillity and a moment of prosperity had returned to the farms of the state by 1919, but the good times were brief. The plummeting of farm prices in 1920 set the stage for another prolonged agricultural depression, for the descent into tenancy and poverty of still more thousands of North Carolinians, and for renewed migration to the cities.

Washington Duke (1820–1905). Ashe,
Biographical History, vol. 3.

Industry Comes of Age

Seed of a Tobacco Empire

Industrialization in North Carolina was not born in the factory but on the farm. It did not begin with clanking machines and a vast hired work force but with laborious hand production by members of the family and a few helpers. A visitor to the homestead of Washington Duke in 1871 caught a glimpse of one of the great industries of the state in its infancy. Taking refuge in the Duke household from a bitter winter storm, the visitor was "hospitably taken into a room with a large open fireplace." While he thawed, he watched Duke's young daughter Mary as she sat at a table and worked. Using the light of a lamp on a day darkened by rain, she filled "little cotton bags from a pile of finely-shredded tobacco before her." When each bag was "stuffed to bursting," she drew it closed "with a sturdy string run through the top and tied it with a bow knot. From time to time she took a pen and wrote in ink 'Pro Bono Publico' on an oblong yellow label which she pasted on the filled bag of tobacco." Totally absorbed by the work, Mary Duke hardly spoke to the visitor.

Within twenty years all would be different. By then, Washington Duke and his daughter and three sons had long since moved to the nearby city of Durham, a hamlet of two hundred and fifty souls in 1870 that grew to a town of thousands by the 1890s. The Dukes and their helpers, once awakened by the crow of the rooster and the glint of the rising sun, were awakened at five in the morning by the factory whistle. Machines had replaced hand manufacture, and advertising had made the Duke name known throughout the world. For thousands of North Carolinians—industrialists, workers, townspeople, farmers—the shift from home industry to mass production reshaped the way they lived.

Washington Duke might have been the last to predict in the late 1850s that he and his sons would preside over a national tobacco empire by the end of the century. A yeoman farmer with three hundred acres, he scratched out a living in cotton and corn, adding a few acres of bright leaf tobacco in the 1850s. The Civil War changed Duke's life. Drafted in 1864 by the faltering Confederate army, the forty-four-year-old Duke served only a few months before capture and spent the remainder of the conflict in a federal prison. Duke was released and shipped to New Bern in 1865. After walking the 135 miles from the coast to home and arriving with fifty cents in his pocket, he discovered that some farmers in the neighborhood were

Washington Duke beside his first tobacco factory. N.C. State Archives. This building is gone, but the Duke Homestead has a replica of it along with other buildings Duke used in manufacturing his tobacco before moving to town.

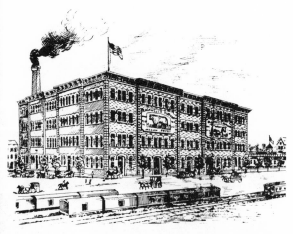

Blackwell's Tobacco Factory. Raleigh *News and Observer*, 5 April 1896. Daily tours of the old Bull Durham factory (Blackwell's), now owned by the American Tobacco Company, 201 W. Pettigrew St., Durham, show the cigarette manufacturing process.

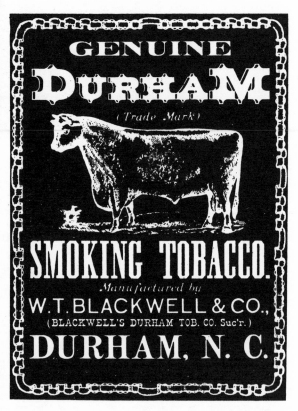

Famous trademark on the label of Bull Durham smoking tobacco. Historic Sites Section, Division of Archives and History.

buying tobacco from their neighbors at six cents a pound, processing it, and selling it at sixty. He decided he had nothing to lose by trying his hand at the manufacture of tobacco.

Duke did not convert his farm to manufacturing overnight, but gradually the family homestead became an industrial plantation. Visible at the Duke Homestead is a small log structure comparable to that which served as the family's first "factory." In such a shed, Duke and his two young sons hand-processed 400 pounds of tobacco a day. Able in 1866 to manufacture and market 15,000 pounds of his brand, Duke converted a nearby stable into a second makeshift factory and in 1873 constructed an authentic two-story wooden factory in which he produced 125,000 pounds of smoking tobacco. Wagonloads of cured and dried tobacco were brought in through its wide doors, hung from tier poles held by the rafters, and kept moist by the opening and closing of small ventilating doors in the attic. The factory's equipment was suited to hand production: flails, sieves, work tables, weights and scales, barrels. By the 1870s young black workers had replaced Duke's teenaged sons at hand labor. Workers flailed the leaves into granules with wooden sticks and then sifted the crumbled leaf through rapidly shaken screens. Duke's helpers and his daughter Mary packed the granulated smoking tobacco into homemade bags and Pro Bono Publico—"For the Public Good"—was ready for sale.

Though Duke's production and sales of smoking tobacco expanded dramatically after 1866, it was clear by the early 1870s that even more remarkable growth was possible for men ambitious enough to gamble high. In 1865 nearby Durham's Station was little more than a railroad depot. By 1874 the town was not only a postwar manufacturing center—with factories, warehouses, a railroad—but it was on the verge of challenging Richmond for tobacco supremacy. Coincidence had helped. In April 1865, while waiting near Durham for the last surrender of the Civil War, troops from both armies had foraged through the area's farms and warehouses, discovered the bright leaf smoking tobacco, and relished it. They wrote back for more after the war. But the real secret of North Carolina's triumph in the tobacco industry was the brash aggressiveness of its new men. Julian Carr, son of a Chapel Hill merchant and co-owner of the W. T. Blackwell firm, which made Bull Durham tobacco, spent an unprecedented three hundred thousand dollars a year to distribute posters and paint signs of a bulgingly virile bull from San Francisco to the pyramids. Simultaneously, Carr offered and paid rewards for new mechanical inventions to increase production and cut labor costs. Triumph came in 1883 to Durham's wizard of advertising when Bull Durham's sales of five million pounds of smoking tobacco became the largest in the nation. The brazenness that built Bull Durham was in the company motto: "Let buffalo gore buffalo, and the pasture go to the strongest."

In 1874 Washington Duke made his decision. He would go for the higher stakes and compete directly with the Bull. Duke moved to Durham and built a new steam-powered factory near the railroad. But, though the locale and the factory were new, Duke's method of production remained traditional. A predominantly black work force of forty adults and twenty children did the bulk of manufacturing by hand. Constructing his personal residence directly across from his factory, Duke essentially transferred the industrial plantation from his homestead to the city.

Competition drove the Dukes to innovate. Despite the expanded sales of the family's smoking tobacco, purchases were far from enough to please Washington Duke's youngest son, James Buchanan Duke. By 1880 the rugged and ambitious "Buck" Duke had had enough of chasing the tail of Bull Durham. In the rivalry for the smoking tobacco market, the Duke company was "up against a stone wall." The younger Duke decided to gamble on a product that had yet to achieve widespread popularity: "I am going into the cigarette business."

Fairview, home of Washington Duke (left); first Duke factory in Durham (left center); and second Duke factory in Durham (right), 1885. N.C. State Archives.

"It was not simply for his [Julian Carr's] factories that the Dukes paid him a million dollars. One might almost say that the factories were thrown in for good measure. It was that trade mark of 'the Durham Bull' which his industrious genius had painted along the highways of all nations which the Dukes knew they must possess, if they would control the tobacco market." Wilson, *Southern Exposure.*

23

James B. Duke (1856–1925). Ashe, *Biographical History*, vol. 3.

Duke of Durham advertisement. Raleigh *News and Observer*, 5 April 1896.

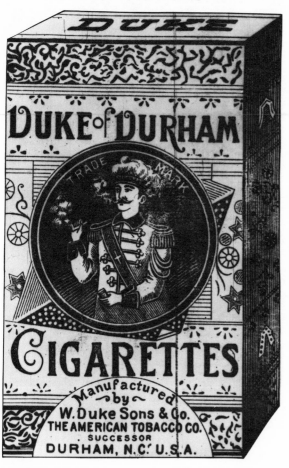

Long popular in Europe, cigarettes began to catch on in the United States toward the end of the Civil War, particularly in larger cities. An alternative to chewing tobacco, cigars, and pipes, the cigarette offered a smoking stimulant suited to a fast-paced urban setting: clean, quick, potent. The manufacture of cigarettes, however, required that each cigarette be hand-rolled. Workers with such skills were plentiful in Europe, rare in America. So in 1881 the Dukes brought to Durham more than a hundred skilled Jewish immigrants, recent arrivals in New York, to practice and teach their trade.

Ironically, the genius of the Dukes and other manufacturers in advertising and promoting their new product soon created a demand for cigarettes that outstripped the capacity of the skilled hand-rollers. In Atlanta an enterprising Duke salesman achieved a coup when he obtained from Madame Rhea, a dazzling French actress, permission to copy a lithograph of her and to show a package of Duke cigarettes in her hand. Sales soared. Coupons for gifts and colorful trading cards soon became standard features of Duke cigarettes: purchasers bought again and again to acquire their prizes and to complete their collections of scantily dressed women, presidents and monarchs, birds and beasts, flowers and fruits. The promotions paid off. Cigarette orders rose to four hundred thousand daily in May 1884. On "the glorious 4th" of July 1884, Duke sales reached almost two million.

Cigarette orders were massive, but Duke's skilled craftsmen could produce only four cigarettes a minute by hand. It was time to mechanize and Duke gambled again. He leased two machines invented by an eighteen-year-old Virginian named James Bonsack. Plagued by imperfections, the complex machine had been tried and discarded by a leading Richmond firm in 1880. Duke and William T. O'Brien, a mechanic sent to Durham by the Bonsack Company, labored for months in 1884 to get the machine to work. They succeeded. By the end of 1884 the Bonsack machine could make two hundred cigarettes a minute at less than half the cost of hand production. James B. Duke moved to New York, set up a second factory there, and relentlessly pursued his ultimate goal. "If John D. Rockefeller can do what he is doing for oil, why should I not do it in tobacco?" Able to control the leasing of the machine through his contract with Bonsack, Duke used all his power to create a monopoly in tobacco. Duke outproduced, outadvertised, and undersold his competitors. Of 253 tobacco factories in North Carolina in 1894, only 33 were left ten years later. The survivors had all become part of the American Tobacco Company, headed by J. B. Duke.

Mechanization revolutionized work and the workplace. The skill and judgment of the cigarette hand-rollers were no longer needed; displaced and embittered, the immigrant craftsmen returned to New York City. The craftsmen were replaced by the Bonsack machines, each of which did the work of forty-eight skilled laborers. The sophistication of the equipment, which can be viewed today in modernized form at tours of major Piedmont factories, was a marvel to behold. Without human intervention it automatically fed the tobacco into the machine, made cigarettes faster than the eye could see, loaded the finished cigarettes onto a tray, packed them into boxes, pasted labels on the packs, and placed the packs into cartons.

So automated was the equipment by 1900 that one worker recalled that "when the work went well, we didn't do a thing!" Only a handful of skilled and highly paid mechanics was needed to repair and maintain the equipment. Others on the cigarette assembly line watched over the machine and corrected its mistakes. When a machine broke down, the worker called a mechanic to mend it. When flawed cigarettes or damaged packages were made, they were removed, taken apart, and reused.

After 1885 demand surged for operatives who could be trained quickly and employed cheaply to tend the machines. Young white men and women from the Piedmont were recruited for the task and seized the chance. Their work opportunities diminished and their marriage prospects blighted by the economic hardships of the countryside, they found in the city the chance for a fresh start and in the factory job the attraction of "making something for myself." Notwithstanding low wages for sixty-five hours a week of work, the "pay seemed like right much" to youths who were not "used to making any money, working on a farm."

Despite the cash wage, some workers were bothered by the loss of independence in the mechanized factory: the "bossing" of the foreman, the endless monotony of the work, the incessant demand to keep pace with the machine, the requirement to stand in place all day. "It aged us before our time," observed a workingwoman. Yet others thought that, despite the machines and the supervision, the tobacco factory floor remained a place of much liberty. They recalled that well into the twentieth century the company's rules were few, the rhythm of work was relaxed, and workers were free to get a drink of water or go to the toilet without first seeking permission. Of course, if you did not like it, as one worker observed, "you could always quit and go to work somewhere else." But for most, quitting was not a genuine option, partly because the wages of other workers —textile operatives and dime-store clerks—were usually lower than those of tobacco factory employees.

Many found that the companionship of fellow employees compensated for the limitations of work and wages. "It was just like a family," one woman recalled. Workers talked to each other above the noise of the machines, exchanged gripes about the foremen, sometimes even sang on the job. In one factory the workers from the entire floor brought their families together on weekends for potluck

The Dukes published a series of actress cards to promote their Cameo brand cigarettes. W. Duke Sons and Co. Papers, Duke University Manuscript Department.

Workers opening hogsheads in warehouse. *Harper's Magazine,* 11 November 1865.

picnics. "We enjoyed it, had a good time." For other employees, company benefits made the job worthwhile. "We had a hospital, a trained nurse, and a doctor who came once a day and prescribed medicine. It was free." For the most faithful employees there were promotions to higher jobs on the factory floor and even desk jobs for those injured at work. But for many the real joy of the job was living in town. There were churches and revivals, department stores and parks, and soon streetcars and electric lights.

For black workers in the tobacco industry of the Piedmont, factory jobs had also brought a vital measure of independence. City labor provided a foothold off the farm, an escape from the grip of tenantry, release from the prospect of lifelong labor behind the south side of a northbound mule.

Mass production in the tobacco factory meant more jobs for blacks, but not better ones. Much of the work once done by black hands became mechanized, and the running of machines was reserved for whites. Left to the black employees was the arduous physical labor of preparing the tobacco leaves for the machines. The factory's leaf department was usually on a separate floor or in its own building. To prevent the drying out of the leaves, windows were often kept closed. In the hot and humid rooms, where the air was sometimes "so heavily laden with fumes and dust" that workers tied handkerchiefs over their nostrils, black women and men sorted and graded the tobacco and removed stems from the leaves. Most blacks recalled their work as hot and "sticky" labor, which bred short tempers. For "doing all the nasty dirty work," black workers were paid little. Black women received half the wages of white women "on the cigarette side" who were able to wear white uniforms on the job. Black men, who made up the gangs that hauled hogsheads of tobacco weighing five hundred pounds to the machine floors, received less than half the pay of white men.

Despite the pay and privation of their labor in the tobacco factories, black workers—like white—found ways to fashion a world they could endure and enjoy. To ease the monotony and enhance the "comradeship" of work, black employees "sang all day long." A man or a woman with a gifted voice would "raise a song"—"it was always spirituals"—and the "whole floor would take up the chant." White passersby and fellow workers found the cadenced chanting "the prettiest thing you ever heard," and even the bosses "used to come out and listen" while hundreds of blacks sang as they worked. Even the insecurity of the job—many blacks were laid off when they completed the preparation of the tobacco leaves—did not diminish the attachment of blacks for their family of fellow workers. "Folks that had laid out would miss it so much until they would be up there at lunchtime." "Nobody had enough to turn anybody's head," one worker summarized. "You enjoyed folks' company more than other assets."

Even in the highly mechanized factory of the early twentieth century, many black and white workers recalled their labor as an "easy-going sort of thing." Ironically, it was the enormous success of the Dukes in tobacco—a field that they dominated by 1899—that set the stage for a pioneering venture that would hasten the end of a genial pace of work in factories throughout the state. The tobacco family took the leadership in the development of hydroelectric power in the region. With increasing wealth at their command by the 1890s, the Dukes began to diversify their investments. They first expanded into the ownership and operation of textile mills and after the turn of the century began to investigate the possibility of tapping the region's cascading rivers—her "white coal"—for industrial use. When James B. Duke asked a brilliant young engineer and future leader of his power company just what a comprehensive plan of development would cost, William S. Lee answered "about $8,000,000. It was the biggest amount I had ever heard of. It seemed to attract him." Incorporated in 1905, the Southern Power Company within the next twenty years built a chain of dams and ten hydroelectric stations from Bridgewater, North Carolina, to Camden, South Carolina. The dams harnessed the entire Catawba-Wateree river system to supply energy for three hundred cotton mills as well as the cities and other factories of the Piedmont. By 1930 Duke Power would be among the largest utility companies in the South.

With the triumph of electricity came the certainty that in a matter of time there would be further mechanization of the factory and acceleration of the pace of work.

The Mill Village

Though small-scale industries existed in North Carolina before the Civil War, it was in the last quarter of the nineteenth century that manufacturing expanded dramatically. The number of cotton textile mills multiplied at a hundred a decade after 1880. By early in the twentieth century, two hundred thousand North Carolinians had moved off farms they had tilled for generations to seek employment in towns or factory villages. For the first time they took jobs for wages, known universally as "public work."

For many, the first public work was in a textile factory, and the first place that they moved to was a mill village. Most of the early factories were located in the Piedmont, where a plenitude of rivers supplied waterpower to drive the machinery of the mills. Factory owners built entire communities in the countryside for their employees and hoped that the rural setting, "comfortable habitations," and neighborliness of village life would ease the transition from farm to factory.

Glencoe, nestled in the heart of the Piedmont, typifies these self-enclosed mill villages. Located three miles north of Burlington, it hugs a gentle stretch of the Haw River, where the original factory still stands. Though the mill ceased operations in the 1950s and though most of the homes and company buildings are no longer in use, Glencoe remains much as it was in the 1880s, when it was constructed by descendants of Alamance County's antebellum textile pioneer, Edwin M. Holt. The mill produced bright and multicolored "Glencoe Plaids" and durable "Deckedout Denim." The mill building, the mill office and company stores, the two-story workers' homes, the village barbershop, and the lodge hall have survived for a century. Some of the land is now overgrown and most of the people are gone, but physically Glencoe remains a classic mill village.

The Holt family, founders of Glencoe and other mills in Alamance County, looked upon their enterprises as more than a means to make a profit. Earnings were not negligible, to be sure. By the 1890s net profits regularly exceeded 40 percent each year and made millionaires of the Holts. But the entrepreneurs who created mill villages in the New South often proclaimed their ventures to be social philanthropy. Factories would redeem the region from the blight of rural poverty and provide deliverance for white youth who might otherwise sink into the "vice of idleness." The cotton mill, they believed, would rescue whole communities from decay, spare the poorest whites from lifelong tenancy, and prevent the plunge of thousands of whites into direct competition with black tenant farmers. All-white mills offered "an escape from competition with blacks" and the means for the moral and material reclamation of the state. It was no wonder that at a revival meeting in Salisbury a preacher holding forth

James H. Holt (1833–97). Ashe, *Biographical History*, vol. 7.

Glencoe, Alamance County, off N.C. #62, is only one of many abandoned mill villages in the state. Others are Coleridge, Randolph County, on the Deep River, built in 1882; and Henry River mill village, off I-40 on S.R. #1803, Burke County, built in 1902. Oakdale Cotton Mills, Jamestown, Guilford County, is still a going concern.

Haw River at Glencoe milldam.

on the plight of the poor declared that the "establishment of a cotton mill would be the most Christian act his hearers could perform." It was in the same spirit that another minister, presiding over the dedication of a new mill in Concord in 1882, celebrated the "roar of the machinery" as "work's anthem to the Lord" and blessed the "smoke from the chimney" as "daily incense to God."

But work alone would not redeem the state or save its indigent from "savagery." Factory owners with a sense of mission sought to create good neighborhoods and well-regulated Christian communities. They attempted to do so, at Glencoe and other mill villages, through paternalism. Paternalism involved in part the physical facilities of the village. At Glencoe the company provided the Union Church, which served Methodists on Sunday mornings and Baptists

Glencoe village house. Note the well at side back; kitchens were originally separate.

Thomas M. Holt Manufacturing Company owned three plants at Haw River. Holt had first bought the old Trollinger gristmill and built the Granite mill in 1844 on that site, parts of which are incorporated in the present structure. Two other mills, the Cora and the Thomas M. Holt, were added in the 1880s and '90s. All are now owned by Cone Mills, Inc.

Ruins of Glencoe church.

in the afternoons. The church building survived until 1976, when it collapsed in a winter storm. A school and a village baseball field were added later at Glencoe; in larger mill villages company libraries, company-sponsored flower gardens, and company auditoriums for entertainment were built to enhance the wholesomeness of the community.

More important to the moral management of the village was the direct interest of the owner in his family of employees. At Glencoe, Robert Holt, son of the founder, lived in the village. He knew all employees and their children by name. Despite Holt's wealth and authority, he seemed "just like one of us," a resident recalled. In other mill villages, owners dispensed paternal gifts. One saw to it that all his female workers received a parasol at Christmas—which he delivered personally from house to house—and chartered a private train for picnic outings on the Fourth of July. Others shared wood or coal with employees in the event of a harsh winter.

But paternalism involved more than gestures of generosity. It also meant control and intrusion. In several villages the patriarch roamed the village at night to make certain that lights were out by 10 P.M. He evicted people who misbehaved and brooked no challenge from "his" people in "his" village. In return for benevolence, the owner expected and often received the loyalty of his employees: a faith that the company would take care of its family of workers and do right by them. Loyalty often diminished the demand for wage increases, as did the custom of renting workers' homes for a dollar a week and providing many village services "free." Few factory owners saw themselves as padding their profits through paternalism. In their view the hard work they required and the moral supervision they provided built character. Employees who labored like the devil were on the road to heaven.

For those who came to Glencoe and to the hundreds of other mill hills that mushroomed in the Carolina Piedmont, the village provided a place of transition to factory life. For many, the change proved relatively easy. Some moved only a short distance from their rural homes. They came with their family or migrated to a community where an older sister or brother was already employed and had recruited them for factory work. To farm people who had worked from sunup to sundown, a dozen hours of factory work a day, six days a week, did not necessarily seem novel or outrageous. Glencoe children—like farm children—began part-time work by ten. At twelve they went full-time and left school forever. Until the first part of the twentieth century, the factory day—like the country day—offered slack time for breaks or sociability. Children who got "caught up" in their work might play outside for twenty minutes in a kind of factory recess; adults could talk while tending the less noisy machines. Unlike the steel factories of Pittsburgh or Birmingham, the

Piedmont mill village remained physically a part of the country. Many companies provided enough land for families to have a garden plot of their own and grass for a cow. Nearby forests remained a hunter's haven for workingmen and their hound dogs.

Yet the transition from farm to mill village was far from easy for all. For some—especially children—the adjustment to factory work could be sudden and startling. The whirring and deafening din of machinery frightened many a novice. One woman recalled that she "fled from the room" with her superintendent in hot pursuit. For children the shock came at the end of the first week's work, with the payment of wages that amounted to 12½ cents a day. "I came home to my momma and I cried," remembered a retired workingman. Nothing on the farm prepared mill workers for the cotton dust of the spinning room, which a Glencoe worker described as "just like a fog." Nor was it easy to adjust to the intense, humid heat of the factory, where moisture was needed to keep cotton fibers from breaking. "You just sweated it out, that's the whole thing there was to it."

Ultimately, many at Glencoe and other textile mills overcame the fear of machinery and factory noise and endured the discomfort of

Glencoe mill workers. Courtesy Alamance County Historical Museum.

Boy from Loray Mill, Gastonia, Gaston County, October 1908. Photograph by Lewis Hine. Edward L. Bafford Collection, University of Maryland Baltimore County Library. "Been at it right smart two years," the boy said.

humidity and heat. But did they also accept other circumstances that had become characteristic of mill village life by 1900—low pay, repetitive work, unchallenged owner control—as conditions that had to be borne with resignation and "just sweated out"? Were they, as textile employers frequently claimed, not only the "cheapest labor market in the United States," but "tractable, harmonious, and satisfied with little," workers who gladly permitted their paternalistic employers "to take care of them" like "children"?

There was much evidence of "adjustment." Having come from a countryside where farms were failing and where women especially were becoming surplus labor, many were simply "glad to be working." Once in the factory, they took immense pride in their work and in their ability to manage the tasks they were assigned. In the early days of factories, an individual tended the same machines every day. It was not unusual for a worker to talk to the machinery, to cajole it, to give it a whack on bad days and praise it on good. For those who tired of the sameness of the work, there was the chance to move around among different jobs at the plant, from doffer to slubber to spinner. Some rose to the supervisory post of foreman, though the distastefulness of pressuring friends and family to speed their work discouraged many from seeking to manage others.

For most who chose to stay at Glencoe and other mill villages, however, it was not so much the rewards of work as it was the familial and neighborly nature of the village that rooted them in place for a lifetime. Many who lived in the community were kin by blood or marriage, and kinship proved important in getting jobs for the young or in taking care of family members when trouble came. One did not have to be blood kin to share the bounty of plenty and the burdens of want. The rule in Glencoe, one workingwoman recalled, was that in good times, "if one's got anything, they divide it," and in hard times, "your trouble's my trouble."

Mill owners found it in their interest to reinforce the bonds of family in the village. Women with young children who wanted to look after their infants might be given piecework that they could do at home, either by hand or with a small machine lent by the company. Because most women had to work full-time—a husband's income was rarely enough to support his family—the company accommodated mothers by permitting them to walk home at midday to feed their family lunch and by allowing them to leave work an hour early in the afternoon to prepare supper. Mill owners used their power as well as their flexibility to give paternal support to the workers' families. They sponsored Sunday schools for the young, penalized severely men who were found drunk, evicted the families of girls who went morally astray, and encouraged foremen to take a "heartfelt interest" in the home lives of employees. More than a few workers recalled such paternal owners with gratitude and affection. "He was our Daddy." "We loved him."

But the familial closeness of the factory employees did not always work to the advantage of the owners or incline the operatives to be "tractable and harmonious." Factory managers anxious to experiment with new methods to spur production complained of the obstructive clannishness of their workers. Employees preferred to "make do" and stick together rather than speed up and compete for higher output and pay. More inclined to "act under clannish impulses" than to submit to the "common sense" of the mill manager, workers "kicked" and "grumbled" and "agitated" when supervisors sought to get strict and impose tighter controls on the job. Complaining of a "great lack of gratitude," managers "reluctantly came to the conclusion that the less employees are interfered with the more content they are." Leaving "employees strictly alone, giving advice only when they ask for it"—"which is very seldom"—management permitted the workers to impose a relaxed pace and neighborly atmosphere on the shop floor.

Eleven or twelve hours of work a day went differently when workers set their own pace. "It was just like a family operation,"

A union organizer recalled his years in factory work: "I like the farm better than the factory any day but on a farm you just work yourself to a frazzle and don't get a thing for it." Banks, ed., *First-Person America*.

A retired worker remembered that in his Glencoe mill days people thought themselves lucky to be working and to have "food on the table, clothes on their back, and a roof over their head."

Zelma Murray, another Glencoe worker, said: "Well, I'll tell you, it used to be that everybody that lived here were kinpeople . . . the superintendent, he was my uncle, he married my father's sister. . . . They were all related some way or another. It might not be close, but most of them were, you know, some kind of an uncle or aunt or some kind of a cousin or something along that line." SOHP.

Women working at the White Oak Mills, Greensboro, ca. 1907. Library of Congress.

recalled one woman. "You had time to fraternize with your fellow workers. You could get up when you had to, sit down when you wanted to." Textile factories required long hours, reflected another worker, "but it was no pressure. When you're working under pressure, it's killing you all the time. We were more like just one big happy family."

Yet for all its expediency—as a racial and economic stopgap for destitute rural whites, as a setting that eased the transition from farm to factory, as a place where family-oriented North Carolinians could resettle in neighborhoods of kin and their own kind—the services of the mill and mill village came at a high price. From the very first, mill owners pledged to prospective investors that "long hours of labor and moderate wages will continue to be the rule for many years to come." From the first they paid wages so low—twenty cents a day for bobbin boys, fifty cents a day for spinners, seventy-five cents a day for weavers—that the entire family was obliged to work in the mills so that they might eat. In 1910 North Carolina textile workers labored ten hours longer each week for 40 percent less than their counterparts in the cotton mills of New England. Under the "family wage" system, the labor of children for the full seventy-hour work week was virtually mandatory. Child labor and low wages took their toll: in illiteracy, in diet and disease, in bodies made "haggard" by prolonged toil from an early age. The separate identity of the mill village was a matter of pride to some. "They provided for us.

We had the best ball fields, the best-dressed ball team. We were the envy" of everyone around. But for others the bleakness and insularity of the village set its residents apart as a distinct caste—"cotton mill folk" and "lintheads"—who were increasingly isolated and socially shunned.

Despite the attempts of the company to create a secure world in the mill village—secure workers, secure families, secure profits—and despite its promise to investors that the "hardy native Anglo-Saxon stock" had "no disposition to strike," there were in fact recurrent symptoms of unrest. Uncertain employment was a chronic difficulty in the 1880s, when a mid-decade depression forced mills to cut production and wages. In response, numbers of Piedmont mill hands affiliated for the first time with a union, the Knights of Labor. They demanded restoration of their wages, reduction of the workweek to sixty-six hours, curbs on child labor, safety inspection, and the creation of a state Bureau of Labor. They nominated their own candidates for state and local offices. The labor ticket almost won in Alamance County against a slate that included several members of the Holt family and briefly succeeded in Durham and Wake counties with the election of the Knights' Master Workman to the state assembly. Alamance mill owner Thomas Holt, who was speaker of the house in 1885 and an aspirant to higher office, responded to the labor ground swell by advocating a state law to limit work to sixty-six hours a week. When the bill failed, he voluntarily cut hours in his own factories—and was in 1888 elected lieutenant governor as the "workers' friend."

Despite extraordinary success in mobilizing three-quarters of a million workers in the nation and thousands throughout the South in the mid-1880s, the Knights of Labor lost its gains by the end of the decade. But the aspirations expressed in the union's very name—*Knights of Labor*—found new ways to flourish in the 1890s. At a time when mechanized factory work and public contempt threatened to degrade manual labor, the Knights had reaffirmed the dignity and "nobility" of human toil. "God was not less because He worked; neither are men." At a time when massive combinations of capital and chronic economic uncertainty rendered individual self-reliance pitifully inadequate as a means of self-protection, the Knights advocated cooperation among workers. Like other organizations that won millions of adherents in the 1880s and 1890s, such as the Farmers' Alliance and the black mutual benefit society, the Knights crusaded for collective action and mutual aid as indispensable means for working people to achieve self-help and reclaim self-respect.

Partly as a result of the Knights of Labor agitation, mill owners of the 1890s were ever alert to stirrings of independence by their workers. As they feared, even in small and paternalistic villages such as Glencoe, there were omens of employee autonomy. In 1896, seek-

Legislation for improved working conditions and fewer hours did not always please the people it was meant to help, according to one mill owner. A bill to stop night work prompted J. S. Ragsdale of Oakdale Cotton Mills, Jamestown, to write to Thomas Settle, his representative in Congress, in 1895: "I have hands from the Reidsville Cotton Mills and from the Greensboro Cotton Mills (both broke and stopped) who came and asked for night work—I went to the expense of Several Thousand Dollars to build houses for them to live in and started a night force who are doing well and well satisfied—work 5 nights a week. My hands unanimously ask that we be not interfered with." Thomas Settle Papers.

ing to make their wages go further, Glencoe's inhabitants deserted the community's company store in favor of merchants miles away who charged a third less for flour, meat, and coal. The mill owner responded with a masterful appeal to company loyalty. Flyers posted all over the village read: "I cannot live without you, or some others like you, and you cannot live without me, or someone like me. Our interests are therefore mutual and the more I make, the better wage I can pay you. You should do what you can to help me."

Notwithstanding such appeals to loyalty, textile unions re-emerged in the state in 1900. The failure of owners to share with wage earners the immense textile profits of 60 percent during the previous year had made the "hardy Anglo-Saxons" of Alamance and other counties receptive to union membership, and hundreds joined. When continued high production glutted the textile market in September 1900 and prompted the Southern Cotton Spinners Association to announce that it would hold the line on prices by curtailing production 40 percent, mistrust of the mill owners and anxiety over impending layoffs reigned in the mills. And yet, in their appeals for membership, union organizers did not press for higher wages or fewer hours. Instead, like the Knights of Labor before them, they urged workers to unionize so as to break their dependency on company goodwill. To "organize themselves for mutual benefit," to "help one another," would be the first step toward regaining their independence as "free men and free women."

It was fitting—and prophetic of the decades ahead—that when protest flared in the fall of 1900 its focus was worker independence. When an unpopular foreman of the Haw River mill challenged a woman weaver for too many trips away from her machine, she defiantly responded that she "would go when she pleased and where she pleased." He fired her on the spot and instructed another woman, described by coworkers as a "powerless orphan," to take her place. Workers in the factory swarmed around the machine, insisted that the foreman had been "rude and unjust," and pressed the young girl to refuse the command. Unable to choose between her job and her fellow workers, she wept. That night the union met, agreed to defy the foreman the next day, and "threw up the machines" when the foreman reissued the order in the morning. Within an hour, the owners shut down the other mills in town.

Workers, mill owners, and editorial writers all recognized that the textile industry and the state had reached an historic crossroad. The mill owners, conveniently overstocked with surplus goods, refused to confer with a committee of the labor union. To "yield to such demands" would "be to give up entire control of the management of the mill on the part of the owners." They posted armed guards around the mills of the county, declared they would operate only with nonunion labor, and ordered all union workers to vacate their com-

Thomas M. Holt Manufacturing Company owned three plants at Haw River. Holt had first bought the old Trollinger gristmill and built the Granite mill in 1844 on that site, parts of which are incorporated in the present structure. Two other mills, the Cora and the Thomas M. Holt, were added in the 1880s and '90s. All are now owned by Cone Mills, Inc.

Company store and office, Glencoe.

pany houses. Union membership promptly soared into the thousands, and the scope of the dispute broadened beyond the issue of employee "liberty" on the shop floor. Did workers and owners, both "citizens of a common country," have an equal right to organize on their own behalf? Could textile workers continue to endure child labor, which mortgaged the futures of the young and eroded the security of the adult?

The union lost, and the workers' reaction to defeat set a pattern for decades to come. Hundreds of "union mill operatives" left the state for South Carolina and Georgia. "Among them," reported the *Alamance Gleaner*, "are a great many excellent people who prefer to go elsewhere rather than surrender rights and privileges which they as citizens deem they should own and enjoy." For the next generation, departure became the textile worker's alternative to acquiescence or protest. Employer complaints of worker "restlessness" grew increasingly shrill; plant managers wrote in despair that their hands were working only four days a week and left on the slightest pretext. Unwittingly the owners themselves had created the conditions that spawned the most nomadic work force in the nation. They chose to invest their profits in the construction of new mills, and the building boom created a labor shortage. Dissatisfied workers, though unable to organize to improve their lot, "didn't have any trouble in getting a job." "If they'd see something they didn't like, all they'd do was haul off and quit, move to the next town, and have a job and a company house, too." As one worker recalled of the early twentieth

Proximity Mill was built in 1898 by the Cone brothers, who carried paternalism further with all kinds of incentives to attract workers. A broadside, ca. 1915, advertised these attractions:

"Mill Runs 60 Hours Per Week
Stops At Noon Saturday
Pays Off 8th and 23rd Of Each Month
Deep Well Drinking Water Pumped
  Through Mill
Have Modern Village: Streets And
  Houses Are Lighted With Elec-
  tricity;
15-Minute Street Car Service To Any
  Part Of The City Of Greensboro;
Good Graded Schools Nine Months Of
  Each Year, Best of Teachers Are
  Employed.
The Health of The People Is Our First
  Consideration."

century, "there was a lot of people moving around in those days." Whatever it expressed—ambition, discontent, "a desire to wander" —the turbulent army of floaters reached almost 40 percent of the textile work force by 1910.

The outbreak of world war in 1914 made more acute than ever the need for a productive and stable textile work force. The war brought a surge in demand for factory goods and—because of a standstill in immigration from Europe—a nationwide shortage of labor. To increase productivity, some North Carolina employers experimented with new methods of "scientific" management, hiring northern superintendents and establishing personnel and cost departments. But many workers resented the "non-productive departments" that siphoned off dollars from their wages, and employers discovered that Yankees had "no idea how to manage Southern workmen." The alternative approach through 1920 was a redoubled employer campaign for "family" loyalty and worker pride. Mill villages were remodeled and modernized. Superintendents and foremen were "picked from the ranks," chosen because they had a "happy way of getting on with people." Often they had "grown up with the people" they oversaw. Revealingly, in the World War I era, workers often referred to their supervisor as "my Uncle." The "Uncle" understood his men, shared their sense of play and fair play, let them out for circuses and fairs, managed their baseball team with enthusiasm and a common love of the sport, and might also be the best fiddler in the factory. His success came not because he was an "order giver" but "because he knows the people and the work; he is part of the family."

The boom in wartime production of textiles brought an increase in the wages and a surge in the aspirations of the state's textile workers. A Greensboro reporter witnessed a scene that seemed to capture the mood of 1920. A mill village couple and their three children stood in front of a Greensboro store window, looking in at a display of silks cascading to the floor. As the woman gazed through the plate glass, "inspecting rich brocades woven for mistresses of empire and broad seas," the reporter detected the "gleam in her eyes." A gleam was all there would be, however. The postwar downturn in demand brought a cut in wages of almost 50 percent, a wave of unsuccessful strikes against the cut, and a return to the patterns of the previous half-century. The year 1929 would bring a decade of renewed struggle to change the status quo, but until and even well after that year the mill and mill village remained largely a place where working people labored for family security that could no longer be found on the farm, compelled to leave the brocades of the New South for others. "I'll never walk no streets of gold here," one woman textile worker concluded, but her consolation was faith. "The Lord is preparing me a place. If I don't get no mansion, I'll get me a place. I can walk the streets of gold up there."

A Railroad Fan's Dream

From its opening in 1896 until the middle of the twentieth century, Spencer Shops—in the words of one of its admirers—was a "railroad fan's dream come true." Located in the Piedmont just two and one half miles northeast of Salisbury—and scheduled to open in the mid-1980s as a state historic site—Spencer was the massive central repair facility of the Southern Railway Company. Southern's thousands of cars and hundreds of locomotives rumbled over 8,500 miles of track that spanned the region from Washington to Atlanta, Charleston to Knoxville, and westward to Birmingham and the banks of the Mississippi River. Crowded into Spencer's 168 acres were locomotives by the scores bustling over miles of yard tracks, an immense roundhouse and turntable, and a five-story Back Shop filled with huge cranes and winches.

Back Shop, Spencer Shops, Rowan County. Note man aloft in center for scale. Historic Sites Section, Division of Archives and History.

Luther Burch, a retired railroad worker, remembered that one of the duties of his first job was to wake up the train crews and engineers when their trains were ready. "They had a boarding house over in East Spencer called the Red Onion . . . they had about thirty to forty rooms I'd imagine." Bluestone, "Southern Railway Company."

View of Spencer Shops from colored
post card ca. 1910. N.C. State Archives.

The small army of laborers who built Spencer Shops in six
months turned open forest and farmland into a clanging workshop
that knew no rest. The sights and sounds were those of energies
that had brought world supremacy to the heavy industry of America
by 1900. Oil, steam, and electricity; the welding of metal and the
clanging of hammer. So the shops throbbed as workmen took tired
equipment, slicked it up, and returned it renewed to the rails. A
panorama of raw energy and engineering efficiency, Spencer was a
sooty spectacle of the New South.

From the sheer power concentrated at Spencer one could understand why the railroad fired the imagination of Carolinians and other
Americans throughout the nineteenth century and into the next. Few
saw the locomotive as a smoke-belching monster that disrupted the
calm of the countryside. On the contrary, the speed and energy of
the railroad held out to every hamlet the promise of growth—outlets
to markets, links to centers of credit, conduits to supplies, and news
from everywhere in the nation. Towns saw in tracks avenues to
greatness, entrepreneurs envisioned iron highways to fortune, and
children heard in steam whistles the call of travel and excitement.
Especially in a state struggling in the 1870s and 1880s for its rightful

share of the wealth of industrializing America, railroads meant progress, profit, and the promise of a better day.

By the time Spencer Shops opened in the late 1890s, railroads in North Carolina and in the South had come of age. The expansion had not been easy. A half-century before, North Carolina had struggled to complete even a few hundred miles of track to connect Wilmington and Weldon on the east coast, and to link the Piedmont towns of Goldsboro, Raleigh, Greensboro, and Charlotte from east to west. In the fifteen years following the Civil War, despite the sale of the state-owned North Carolina Railroad to the larger Richmond and Danville line, little of the private capital needed for expansion could be found

Southern Railway engine, 1904 model. N.C. State Archives.

John Steele Henderson (1846–1916). Ashe, *Biographical History*, vol. 1.

in the state or lured from outside. But between 1880 and 1890 investment poured into North Carolina and railroad mileage more than doubled.

As railroads crisscrossed the state, pounded into reality by "gangs of sweating blacks and whites who cut and graded and bridged their way" across the Piedmont and the Appalachians, the hopes of many Carolina towns and individuals were realized. Not the least of those fantasies was that of John Steele Henderson, who received advance word in 1895 of the plans of the Southern Railway to build a repair facility near Salisbury and persuaded the rail trust to locate the shops on land he owned or promptly bought up from black farmers. As his wife wrote their daughter, "Mr. H— is selling a small amount of his land for the shops proper and that at a mere nominal price, but the great advantage is that his land surrounds all this spot." A "town of several thousand inhabitants is obliged to spring up right there." When the secret got out, the people of Salisbury shared in the landowner's excitement. There was "great talk of electric lights or of extending Main Street out to the Shops or having electric cars." The delight of one citizen kept him "drunk for two days." Townspeople had "very little money," Mrs. Henderson reported, but "great expectations."

In full operation by the turn of the century, Spencer Shops was a victory for the values of the industrialized age. Just as trains ran round the clock, so the repair shops operated day and night. Light and energy came continuously from the nearby electric powerhouse. In the still competitive railway industry of the early twentieth century, reliability and promptness remained imperative, and the Spencer work force supplied both. Despite the large amount of equipment sent for repair—by the 1930s the figure reached seventy locomotives and forty freight and passenger cars per day—the mechanics of the shops developed a national reputation for the unfailing skill and speed of their workmanship. To minimize the turnover of its skilled employees, the company sold homes and house lots at a low profit and contributed annually toward the operation of the town's churches and YMCA.

But railroad tracks brought trials as well as blessings. As ever larger corporations bought local railroad lines and consolidated them, the state and its citizens surrendered control over rates, services, and schedules to outsiders. Customers might benefit temporarily from rate-cutting wars and from the competitive duplication of tracks, but more often they found themselves without recourse when railway firms resorted to rate fixing and mergers to curtail "cutthroat" competition.

The Southern Railway and Spencer Shops were themselves the result of a successful effort to consolidate and control a bankrupt earlier line. The predecessor line had overbuilt and nakedly plundered

Unidentified railroad accident. N.C. State Archives.

its stockholders during the railroad boom of the 1880s. Incorporated in 1894, the Southern was ruled by a Georgia-born engineer, with a degree from the University of Virginia, who in the eighties was president of the Baltimore and Ohio (B&O). But the Georgian— Samuel Spencer—had left the B&O in 1889 to join the New York banking house of J. P. Morgan. It was from New York that Morgan and Spencer made the decision to locate the line's repair shops in North Carolina—and all other decisions as well. The farmers of the Tar Heel state, first to feel the squeeze of rates they felt discriminatory, fought successfully for a railroad regulatory commission in the early 1880s. But not until the first decade of the next century, when urban leaders took up the reform, was an effective commission created.

Well into the twentieth century, Spencer Shops flourished as a double-edged emblem of power. It pulsated with the new energies that the railroad had released within the state. And it stood for the profound power of corporations to shape the fate of North Carolinians from outside.

The wreck of the Old '97 occurred near Danville, Virginia, in 1908 when this Southern Railway train was on its way to Spencer.

"They handed him his orders at Monroe, Virginia,
Sayin': 'Pete, you're way behind time.
This is not Thirty-eight, but it's old Ninety-seven;
You must put 'er in Spencer on time!'"

Prince, *Southern Railway System.*

Greensboro parade, 1908, going down
Elm Street. N.C. State Archives. Note
Proximity Mills float in center.

The Urban Magnet

The late nineteenth century was the age of the metropolis in the United States. Great cities emerged in the Northeast, along the Great Lakes, and in the Far West. The population of the cities exploded, enlarged in part by the natural increase of large urban families, and swollen enormously by massive migrations from rural America and from Europe. Ethnic enclaves emerged and class disparities widened, as the metropolis spawned both dense slums and astonishing fortunes. For better and for worse, the urban centers of the nation became meccas for millions.

In the mushrooming of the nation's metropolises, no North Carolina city joined. There were only six towns with populations over ten thousand at the turn of the century, and the state's largest city in 1920 had just over thirty thousand souls. Yet, during the fifty years from 1920, a steady evolution and cumulative change was evident. Towns and small cities became magnets for the ambitious and the restless, as well as havens of hope for those forced off the land by rural poverty. Decade by decade, more North Carolinians made town their home: one in twenty-five in 1870, one in ten in 1900, one in four by 1930.

Of course, there were small towns in North Carolina before 1870, but not all were to expand after the Civil War. Absolutely essential for growth was a railroad line. Then a town might add tobacco factories, as did Durham and Winston, or become the center for the textile industry, as did Greensboro or Charlotte. With a railroad connection, Tarboro could expand as a marketing center for cotton and tobacco, and Hamlet could become a flourishing junction for passengers of the Seaboard Railroad Line.

Yet, while the luck of location and a railroad line were factors in deciding whether or not a town got ahead, so were pluck and energy. At least so thought a native North Carolinian who traveled the state in 1884. Walter Hines Page, who would later go on to become the editor of the *Atlantic Monthly* and American ambassador to Britain during World War I, thought that there were two types of Tar Heel towns in the 1880s. Some remained in the grip of the past, their sleepy tone and leisurely habits set by former planters. In such languishing villages, there was "little animation in man or beast. The very dogs look lazy." Other towns were hubs of enterprise, with reputations for business and energy. They sported "no professional talkers and habitual loafers." It was in these go-ahead towns, which were smaller in scale but identical in ambition to the dynamic cities of

Hamlet Depot, Richmond County, built in 1900. A variety of railroad stations from the period remain. These include: Thomasville Depot, Davidson County, 1870; Washington Depot, Beaufort County, 1904; Tarboro Depot, Edgecombe County, 1908; and Concord Depot, Cabarrus County, 1913.

45

George Black. Wilson, *George Henry Black*. At 100 years of age he remembered with tears his frustrated early ambition: "I wanted to go to school real bad."

When Colonial Williamsburg, where Black had worked in the 1930s, asked him in his nineties to help set up a brickmaking exhibit, "he got down in the pit with the young workers to show them how to do it, and he almost worked them to death." Wilson, *George Henry Black*.

the North and the Midwest, that money was pursued without shame, that idleness was scorned, and that the ideology of progress took root.

The Call of the City

The career of George Black illustrates the difference a town could make in the life of a young man. The mud-daubed timber of a log cabin in Randolph County and the sun-dried bricks of the sidewalks of restored Old Salem appear to have nothing in common. But they share something vital: the skills and drive of a family that moved from country to city.

George Black's grandmother and father were slaves. After emancipation his father acquired five acres of land on his former master's plantation, built his own cabin, and began a free life for his growing family. As a home for two parents, a grandmother, and four boys who shared the same rope bed, it was crowded. Everyone in the household worked. Black's pipe-smoking grandmother, who would live to the age of 117, did laundry for white families. His father raised wheat and cut cords of timber that he sold for firewood. Typically, the Black family could not spare its children for education. Enrolled in the cramped colored school for what seemed like only a few months—long enough to learn his alphabet—George Black was called back to labor in the fields. What life would have held for him had George Black and his family stayed on the farm is uncertain.

Chance brought George Black and his family to Winston and fused their fates with the bricks that built the city. His father walked to Winston in 1889 to bring back George Black's half brother who had moved earlier to the town and started to "run wild." A brickmaker offered work to the father and his two sons, and he accepted. But he did not return to Winston until winter, and then discovered that brickmaking was a seasonal trade and that the kiln was closed until spring. City Negroes mocked the farmer's ignorance, but he stayed and brought his family to town. In 1890 George Black's father died, but the family remained. Eleven people lived in their one-room rented tenement and all who could worked. George and his brother Will took jobs hauling bricks at twenty-five cents a thousand. Their daily journeys began at the mud-mill, where the bricks were made in molds, and dozens of times a day they carried the molds to pallets to dry.

One day George Black told his brother: "They can pay us pretty good money, we do the work, and they make more money than we make. How come we can't make brick and get it all?" His brother doubted that white people would buy brick from colored men. Undaunted, George Black "slipped out and built a brickyard to myself.

When I got off work, I'd go work in my brickyard." Customers bought all he could make, and, after selling the first hundred thousand, he went into business for himself full time. George Black's own children helped him as soon as they grew old enough, just as he had helped his father on their Randolph County farm. The quality of Black's work was first-rate. All the bricks on the sidewalk in Old Salem, as well as those of its market firehouse are his. His energy became legendary: he regularly made seven thousand bricks a day.

Town life had unleashed the energy of George Black. There he acquired a marketable skill, started a business, prospered, and won admiration. Said this son of a slave to his brother: "I told you if we made men out of ourselves people would call us Mr. Black."

Main Street

A vigorous middle class prospered in North Carolina's towns and created and supported a diverse array of stores and services. Carolinians who once had bartered for their goods at the antebellum gristmill or who had traded for necessities at the postwar country store, now had new options. At the Briggs Hardware Store in downtown Raleigh, for example, the customer found everything in the hardware line. A large sign and tantalizing wares at the entrance drew the shopper into T. H. Briggs's four-story red-brick store, in 1874 "the tallest building in East Carolina and Raleigh's first skyscraper." The buyer might gossip for a few minutes and warm himself by the stove, but there was rarely the marathon of talking that characterized the country store. The order was placed, service was prompt, the purchase was made. Part of the pleasure in the high-ceilinged store, with its skylight letting in shafts of sunshine from above, was watching the clerk roll the wooden ladder to just the right place, climb high, and pluck down the merchandise in the quantity desired. Even though it was a store of staples, Briggs—like most enterprising merchants— always stocked the new and the novel and invited his customers to try "the latest."

Just as Briggs offered his Raleigh buyers both the novel and the basic, so the town drugstore offered an array of the essential and the newfangled. Often the drugstore was an elegant little emporium, such as Fordham's of Greensboro. With its marble counters, gilded mirrors, and elaborate iron grillwork, Fordham's doubled as an ice-cream parlor. Frequently, it attracted ladies who dressed fashionably for the occasion of an afternoon chocolate sundae. Fordham's main business was medical nostrums, some to cope with timeless maladies, others to alleviate ailments accentuated by life in the town. "Hall's Hair Renewer" promised to thicken "The Growth of the Hair" and to retard

Old view of Briggs's, Raleigh, Wake County. N.C. State Archives. Also a construction business, Briggs's was responsible for building many houses in Oakwood, then a new residential area of Raleigh.

A Briggs ad in 1887 listed, among the wares, builders' supplies, house furnishing goods, stoves, ranges, sporting goods, guns, paints, oils, varnishes, and wagon and buggy materials. *City of Raleigh.*

baldness. Lydia Pinkham's Vegetable Compound—21 percent alcohol —offered the "ultimate remedy for female complaints." Remedies for dyspepsia abounded.

Drugstore proprietors frequently were more than passive dispensers of prebottled elixirs. Some invented stimulants and cures of their own. In 1896 New Bern pharmacist Caleb Bradham devised the formula for a revitalizing soft drink and gave the world Pepsi-Cola. In turn-of-the-century Durham, where young blades felled by hangovers staggered to the drugstore of Germain Bernard, they obtained relief that "worked in minutes." When Commodore Thomas Council put up the capital to market the remedy nationwide, customers everywhere could buy BC Powder. Salisbury druggist Tom Stanback invented his patent medicine in 1911, and sufferers have since been able to "Snap Back with Stanback."

Even in smaller hamlets, where there was no great gusto for becoming the next Chicago, there developed a lively passion for growth. Towns such as Henderson and Tarboro became meeting points between the local rural world and a wider urban one. The ambitious young man who wanted to live in a community with a courthouse square, a newspaper, at least one drugstore, two doctors, and several banks could find himself a delightful town without difficulty and flourish there. He might come to Oxford and enter

Its original sign still marks an old drugstore in Whiteville, Columbus County.

The Vick Chemical Company, Greensboro, was the creation of Lunsford Richardson, a Davidson graduate, who began as a self-taught pharmacist. He developed Vick's Vaporub in 1912, a product that the 1918 flu epidemic made a household word.

"An American woman who respects herself . . . must buy something every day of her life. If she cannot do it herself, she must send out some member of her family for the purpose." Henry James, *An International Episode* (New York, 1879).

(Opposite) Fordham's Drugstore, Greensboro, Guilford County. Photograph by Joann Sieburg-Baker. N.C. State Archives.

Zollicoffer's Law Office, Henderson, Vance County.

Statesville's 1892 courthouse and post office, now the city hall, Iredell County. Union County Courthouse, 1886, at Monroe, conveys the dignity and rich embellishment of the late Victorian era. Clay County Courthouse, 1888, at Hayesville, creates the same effect.

business on College Street—still a perfectly charming townscape of turn-of-the-century America. Or he might, as did A. C. Zollicoffer in 1882, go to Henderson.

A. C. Zollicoffer moved from Halifax County to Henderson at the age of twenty-eight to open up a law practice and soon hung his shingle on the small Main Street office that has remained in the family for three generations. Much of his practice focused on the usual staple of the law—deeds and defaults, battery and bankruptcy—and he spent as many hours with red, leather-bound, oversized mortgage books as he did palavering in his office with clients. Zollicoffer's comfortable and habitable office, and his reputation as an attorney who could skillfully litigate a suit but who preferred to negotiate a settlement, won him loyal clients over the years. It was a measure of the lawyer's standing and the community's enterprise that he also represented the town's largest corporations: its textile mill, bagging company, and biggest bank.

Many middle-class residents of modest towns were like Zollicoffer. Not out to make a fortune, they practiced their professions or trades and led a full life in a small place. The most successful families enjoyed ownership of "beautiful residences," with "houses set back in tremendous yards, some of them full of great magnolias and evergreen trees." For ladies there were afternoon teas and Wednesday meetings of the literary society. The pleasures of daily sociability, the barbs of local gossip, sheltered innocence and Gothic intrigue—small-town life looked uneventful only to the outsider. The high point of the week usually came each Friday night and Saturday, when a full tide of humanity swept in from the surrounding area and filled Main Street with customers and peddlers, carriages and wagons.

Town growth made possible a burst of civic enterprise. The new courthouse at Statesville, built in 1889 after the old one had burned, was massive and solid and mirrored the pride of the town. More than a monument, the new courthouse provided an organic center of town life. Before and after transacting civic business, people met and chatted on the courthouse lawn and sat and gossiped on the hallway benches. The town hall of Apex, Wake County, built in 1912, marked the growth to five hundred residents of a locale that got its name in 1873 for being reputedly the highest point on the railroad run between Norfolk and Sanford. The town government made the most of its new municipal building. The first floor served as a farmers' market, with two rooms given over to fruit and vegetable bins and four designated as butcher shops. A first-floor room measuring sixteen-feet square was set aside as the jail, divided into one cell for each race. (Members of the Baldwin Gang, notorious bootleggers who operated out of Apex after state prohibition passed in 1907, spent little time in the jail.) The mayor's office on the upper story stood alone in the front corner of the building, while the remainder of the second floor housed the town theater, with an ample stage, side dressing rooms, and "opera seats" for the audience.

Town growth meant hazards as well as amenities. Polluted water, offensive smells, the danger of epidemics, were among the new risks that townspeople had to face and overcome. Communities slowly moved from haphazard provisions made by volunteers or private companies to systematic municipal services. To keep a fire from becoming a conflagration—which nonetheless happened frequently—volunteer bucket brigades were replaced with professional firemen. Towns such as Henderson bought new equipment and housed it in new brick firehouses with high belltowers. Often a disaster—such as the failure of a privately operated water system during a fire or an epidemic linked to open pigpens and the lack of a health department—created a demand for a professional manager to assume control over city affairs. "The day of the specialist, the expert, and system has come," said one exasperated alderman. The time of "the old slip-shod jack of all trades method has passed."

Not all the hazards of North Carolina's emerging towns and cities were physical. Moral perils lurked as well, at least in the view of those individuals who belonged to the powerful genteel culture of the late nineteenth century. Many of the communities that became cities at the turn of the century began as industrial frontier towns and attracted large numbers of single young people. When available, work was heavy, demanding more than sixty hours a week from most laborers. But employment was also erratic and seasonal. For those with or without work, emotional release was imperative. It was no

Henderson Fire Station, Vance County, built in 1908.

Raleigh Fire Department, Wake County, 1890, with the champion volunteer Rescue Steam Fire Engine Company. Photograph by Will Wynne. N.C. State Archives.

Carrington's Bar, Durham, possibly ca. 1890. Duke University Manuscript Department. Carrington's ad said: "Carrington don't advise you to drink, but if you will drink he will supply you with pure liquors." Durham *Tobacco Plant*, 22 February 1882.

Unidentified charmer. Courtesy Eno River Association, Hugh Mangum Collection.

surprise that Charlotte had fifteen saloons in the 1880s and that Durham, Winston, and Greensboro were not far behind. Saloons soon created problems. Ladies were annoyed by loiterers. Brawls in bars spilled out into the streets. Clergy began to condemn the saloons as the "spring traps of hell, the devil's octopus, reaching out to grasp the young men of the community."

Prostitution flourished along with the liquor trade. On occasion a respectable woman admitted fascination with the afternoon "promenade down Main Street" of a famous town prostitute. Gorgeous, tall, eyes glittering, her superb figure outfitted fashionably, the voluptuous lady seemed haughty with the knowledge that she could blackmail half the men in town. But those who were fascinated were outnumbered by those who were repelled or resentful. By the turn of the century, many women and impressive numbers of men joined in crusades to close the bars and brothels. In town after town they sent the rowdies packing and cleansed the city—at least to the extent of eradicating the prominent buildings that were once palaces of forbidden pleasure.

Once the turn-of-the-century town was domesticated, it became a special haven for women of leisure. As shoppers, they could stroll down Main Street, their long skirts swishing up the dust, and enjoy the courtesies of men doffing their fedoras and offering a courtly "good afternoon." They could stop at their favorite dry goods store, exchange juicy bits of news with saleswomen, and choose from bolts of cloth their favorite material to be made into a garment at home or by a dressmaker. One of the great treats was a visit to the millinery shop. None remains today, but what exotic sights they were in their time. Perched high on pedestals, hats were festooned with colorful feathers, flowers, or fur, ribbons, ruches, or ruffles. To walk through the store was like "strolling through a flower garden." For a youngster, the trip to town might climax with a visit to the candy store, often run by immigrants. There one could savor a chocolate nougat and be enraptured by the sight and smell of sweet syrup boiling in great copper kettles and by the strenuous wonders of the taffy-pulling machine.

When hats were hats. Courtesy Eleonore Alexander.

Victorian Homes

The widening network of railroads, the dramatic expansion of industry, and the gradual growth of towns and cities brought a new measure of well-being to middle- and upper-class North Carolinians. Reflected in proud new civic and commercial buildings, that wealth also found expression in private residences and suburban development. Though quite different from each other, the Propst House of Hickory and "Körner's Folly" of Kernersville, the suburb of Dilworth in Charlotte and the R. J. Reynolds country estate in Winston-Salem, all illustrate shared principles of design that became common after 1880 in homes of the prosperous. Each offered a more spacious enclave for family privacy, and each presented a vivid architectural display of newfound wealth.

The Propst House of Hickory is the stuff of which nostalgia is made. There is a lightness, an airiness, a genteel whimsy about the late-Victorian dwelling. It is more than fantasy, more than a languid longing for a simpler age gone by that endows this late-Victorian home with its aura of charm. The house was designed by Mr. Propst himself, who erected it between 1881 and 1885.

A skilled builder and wood-carver, J. Summie Propst followed the latest in Victorian fashion in constructing the house. Abundant windows, each framed and set off with elaborate gingerbread fretwork, gave the home almost two dozen eyes to the world. The windows in turn opened the interior of the house to light and shifting shadows at all times of the day. Distinctive about the Propst House is its French mansard roof and tower, stylish signs of elegance and cosmopolitanism. Though the style suggests quality and refinement, the overall effect of Propst's house design is not pompous but playful. The eye dances up the tower, lingers on its hand-carved woodwork, and then easily imagines itself inside the cupola, secretly espying the

Propst House, Shuford Memorial
Gardens, Hickory, Catawba County.

world from behind lace curtains. The detailed exterior decoration is emblematic of the late-Victorian house itself—full of crannies and nooks, carved curls and crevices, the very opposite of spare and symmetrical. The furniture, the objets d'art, even the wallpaper and carpeting, reinforce the motif of whimsy and embellishment in space and design.

It was no accident that such a stylish and spacious house, done in the fashionable Second Empire motif, had arrived in the tiny hamlet of Hickory in 1880. The coming of the railroad to town in the previous decade had brought new prosperity and put the community's home builders and buyers directly in touch with the latest trends of the era. On the railroad came the newest pattern books for homes. At sawmills nearby or far away, orders could be placed for elaborate manufactured moldings, factory-produced woodwork and doors, even for entire stairways. Carolina's traditional house—box-shaped, two-story—gave way to homes more modish and decorative. The sovereignty of skilled local builders like Propst, who could carve elegant ornamental work by hand, yielded to builders whose task was largely one of assemblage. For the rising middle class of the state's small towns, the easy access and ready assembly of manufactured building materials brought the latest in fashion within their reach. Though the Propst House has been relocated to a city park, its original setting was both apt and typical. The house was built so that its front faced the railroad tracks.

A plenitude of space was as much a hallmark of the Propst House as fashionable good taste. Though the Hickory dwelling did not have the endless maze of rooms that distinguished the mansions of the rich—separate rooms for billiards, smoking, sewing, piano, library, servants, greenhouse—it had more rooms and roominess than the typical antebellum home. Working and eating, sleeping and sewing, no longer had to take place in the same multifunctional chambers. Each person and most activities had discrete quarters of their own. The spaciousness of the home was thought to be an important aid to domestic affection. Family members could gather comfortably on the porch, in the parlor, around the piano, near the fireplace, and warmly share each other's company. Yet there was also privacy to be had in the house; each had a room of his or her own.

At first glance the home of Jules Körner of Kernersville, about ten miles east of Winston-Salem, seems to deserve the name given to it by contemporaries: Körner's Folly. Built in 1880, the three-

Interior of Propst House, showing bead and dowel work.

Körner's Folly, Kernersville, Forsyth County. Photograph by Randall Page. N.C. State Archives.

St. Paul's Methodist Church, 1879, Randleman, Randolph County, now the North Randolph Historical Society Museum, was decorated by Körner.

Living room at Körner's Folly. Photograph by Randall Page. N.C. State Archives. The mixture of styles, materials, and designs suggests eccentricity run wild.

story, twenty-two-room residence spreads every which way. A multiplicity of heights and levels and a myriad of building materials give it the appearance of a miniature castle, misbegotten in stone, wood, and eight different sizes of handmade brick. Its sharply pitched roof swarms with spirelike chimneys; recessed arches and narrow windows endlessly ornament the facade.

The interior of Körner's singular dwelling is even more eclectic. There are seven levels in the house, connected by a maze of halls and winding stairways. No two doors are of the same dimensions. The master bedroom features twelve-foot ceilings, the children's playroom six, while other rooms soar to heights of nineteen to twenty-five feet. First-floor rooms have walls paneled with silk, floors of marble and handmade tile, and lavishly carved woodwork. An elegant reception room is crowded with statuary and overstuffed chairs, its walls decorated by hand-painted murals and frescoes. The Körners' bedroom, forty-two feet long, once held thirty-one paintings and a heaven of velvet carpets. Its walls were bordered with Greek designs of love and marriage, and its three chandeliers were suspended by brass cupids. A soaring room on the third floor, first used for billiards, became a family music room and then a little theater —called "Cupid's Park"—for the performance of plays written by Mrs. Körner. Even the home's adjacent pigpen was built of brick and frescoed inside.

The home seems the perfect expression of Körner himself. A richly successful commercial artist, he "traveled widely, painted everywhere"—"even on the Rock of Gibraltar," according to one account. His nom de plume was "Reuben Rink," and his most renowned and lucrative portraits were those of the Durham Bull, world-famous symbol of the state's leading tobacco manufacturer in the 1880s. The eccentric Körner relished his reputation for oddity. One oft-repeated tale had it that he periodically donned the clothes of a handyman, stood at the foot of his "Folly," and invited comment about the structure. "Vulgar" and "deranged" were some of the ready replies.

"Körner's Folly" was idiosyncratic, yet in many ways it was also the extreme culmination of widespread aspirations and possibilities in residential designs of late nineteenth-century America and Europe. Beginning in the 1830s and with increasing audacity and velocity after 1860, Victorian home builders spurned the rules of beauty of the classical style. Order and harmony, symmetry and proportion, had governed the design and decoration of classical dwellings and were characteristic of antebellum plantation homes and their furnishings. But in a world galvanized by manufacturing, crisscrossed by railroads, and connected by steamers and telegraphs, a deep restlessness prevailed. A hunger for novelty brought an impatience with the "monotony" of the older beauty and a quest for styles more suited to the exuberance and power of an imperial age.

No single new style emerged to displace the classical. Instead, diverse architectural forms came to have equal prominence. Buoyant variety, ever more elaborate ornamentation, and a striving for surprise became the hallmarks of external design in the late nineteenth century. By the time Körner built his house, complete irregularity

Körner's dining room. Photograph by Joann Sieburg-Baker. N.C. State Archives. Körner seems purposely to have violated principles of symmetry, proportion, and harmony. (Below) A Körner sampler. Photograph by Randall Page. N.C. State Archives.

Gingerbread on an Oakwood house, Raleigh, Wake County. Oakwood is a kaleidoscope of residential styles from the 1870s to the first decades of the present century. Piazzas, turrets, gables, cupolas, bay windows, and French doors produce an exuberant mix.

The Historic District of Tarboro, Edgecombe County, with houses mostly from 1880 to 1920, supplies another townscape of the period.

was the "rule." Residential facades had different elevations; roofs had ridges and turrets. The same dwelling was finished in wildly diverse materials, such as brick, stone, shingle, timber, and slate. Homes had porches and balconies, overhangs and towers, transparent bay windows and resplendent stained glass.

In part, the architectural asymmetry of Körner's home and others' was the result of a new principle of house design. Those who could afford it built from the inside out, not from the outside in. No longer need the owner subordinate his wish for comfort and convenience or his fancy for specialized rooms to the confining dictates of external symmetry. If separate rooms were wanted for smoking, for billiards, for a library, for music, as well as for sleeping and entertaining and dining, so be it. Let the exterior shape of the house be improvised around the expansive demands for varied rooms.

Clearly at work as well was a relentless desire for display and conspicuous consumption. The new rich had wealth beyond the dreams of their forebears, fortunes built on the enterprises and national markets of the industrial age. With no income taxes to tithe away their profits, with minimal government services to support, they could afford splendid monuments to their new wealth. Home and possessions announced social arrival and set the pace in fashionable taste.

Yet the elaborateness of home and furnishings involved more than a battle for social position among the monied few. Landscaped grounds, picturesque dwellings, boldly patterned wallpaper, flowered carpets, looping drapery, and curvaceously carved and tufted furniture doubtless provided an oasis of enchantment to counteract much of the drabness of the industrial scene. The very mechanization that was the taproot for new fortunes served to reduce the cost of art and adornment and to bring scaled-down Victorian elegance and embellishments within reach of a growing middle class. Mechanized printing presses turned out pattern books for the construction of Victorian residences (and stables and even jails). Machines produced shutters and railings, roofing slates and floor tiles, and prefabricated gingerbread trim in endless variety and profusion. From machines came an outpouring of statuary, pictures, vases, flower bowls, carpets, and upholstered furniture. The less costly the adornments, the more they flourished—and propelled the wealthy to more dramatic display.

One man's fantasy? Körner's Folly was surely that. But his defiantly individualistic and whimsical dwelling also captured the aspirations of an entire new class of entrepreneurs determined to break past old boundaries of wealth and taste alike.

Suburban Sanctuary

The United States census of 1890 officially designated as a "city" any community that had over twenty-five hundred persons within its boundaries. North Carolina had a handful of such cities as the decade of the nineties opened, none of them populated by more than ten thousand souls. Yet in 1891 an aggressive forty-one-year-old entrepreneur from Charlotte, Edward Dilworth Latta, announced that his newly formed Charlotte Consolidated Construction Company planned to develop a suburban community at the southern outskirts of the city on a rural site that had formerly been the city fairgrounds.

The suburb of Dilworth was to be a "city of Avenues." A three-mile boulevard 100 feet wide would encircle the suburb; avenues 60 feet wide were to crisscross the development. There would be 1,635 lots in all, each "beautifully laid off." The centerpiece of the suburb was to be a picturesque park, also named after the developer. In Latta Park fountains would be everywhere, flinging "their spray in an atmosphere laden with the fragrance from thousands of rare flowers and costly roses." The park would have a lily pond, terraced gardens, serpentine paths for promenades, and meandering drives for carriage rides. It would have a lake for boating and a spacious pavilion for light entertainment.

How would visitors get to the park, and, more importantly, how would residents make the daily four-mile round trip to town? With ease. All would travel on the new marvel of urban transport, the electric trolley. "Clanking, pounding, groaning on curves, audible for blocks," popping blue sparks at the switches and providing hazardous mirth for youths who jerked the trolley pole away from the overhead cable, the electric streetcar first proved its success in Richmond in 1888. It sparked emulation and spurred suburban development nationwide for the next three decades. The Charlotte trolley line and parent electric company, like Dilworth and its glistening park, were constructed, owned, and operated by the Latta corporation.

But did a North Carolina city of ten thousand need a suburb that could house ten thousand? A Charlotte journalist would later wonder whether the laying of trolley tracks, creation of suburbs, and erection of skyscrapers were a megalomaniac fantasy of "little more use" to a small Carolina town "than a hog has for a morning coat." Latta and his partners in the "4C's" company anticipated and brusquely dismissed such doubts. The only way Charlotte and the state could break decisively from a past of poverty was to emulate the dynamic urban society of the North. "We must go forward or retrograde," Latta declared. "There is no resting point with progress." Suburban development would inaugurate the "march of improvement."

And so the laying out of Charlotte's first suburban paradise for the middle class got under way. Free picnics in the park, boisterous

Edward Dilworth Latta (1851–1925). *National Cyclopaedia of American Biography*, vol. 20.

A longtime resident, Miss Elizabeth Williams, described Dilworth as a "good place to live." Latta, she explained, "envisioned a balanced community with manufacturing, with all the public facilities necessary, with recreational facilities, with streets laid out and homes built according to certain restrictions." Interview by Elizabeth Turner.

Latta Arcade, 1914, Charlotte, built by Latta to house his 4Cs company office as well as a number of shops. The exterior is badly altered, but the interior, with its marble walls and floors, carved woodwork, and leaded glass, retains its original elegance and simplicity. The concept of shops opening on an inner hall is the ancestor of the shopping mall plan.

The 1880s saw a decided improvement in the quality of city life. Frame buildings gave way to brick or stone, sewerage and telephone systems were introduced, horsecars provided cheap transportation, and electricity replaced gaslight along the streets.

baseball games, and colorful balloon ascensions lured curious citizens out to the treeless countryside for Dilworth's first land sales. Boys with red flags marked the boundaries of the lots, and a bellowing auctioneer took buyers' bids. From 1891 to 1893 sales went slowly, perhaps because prospective buyers did not yet share the vision of the promoters, perhaps because they lacked the ready cash to plunk down for a lot and the construction of a home. But with the trolley in place, the park in use, and the decision of the developers in 1893 to offer low-interest home loans, purchases accelerated.

More fundamental forces favored Dilworth's ultimate success. The promise of shady tree-lined streets, away from the tensions of the city and close to the country, had long since demonstrated a deep appeal to Americans. The suburban home represented a retreat from the world of commerce, and nearby nature was a reinforcement for domesticity. The slogan of Dilworth and hundreds of other budding suburbs—"Why Rent When You Can Own Your Own Home?"—had immense power with the growing middle class, eager to become men and women of property. The promise of space and privacy, the security of a neighborhood made up of one's own kind—those who had the time and the money to trolley to work—seemed more credible in the suburb than in the city, with its crowding and clamor of classes. And Dilworth offered its residents the most modern conveniences: running water, electricity, a new sewerage system, incandescent street lamps, and a spanking new school.

The isolation of Dilworth from the industrial city was not complete, however, as it would be for most later suburban developments. Dilworth was adjacent to a small, suburban industrial community. The industrial park was built by Daniel Tompkins, Charlotte textile manufacturer and publisher of the *Charlotte Observer*, who was widely regarded as a leading spokesman for the New South. The industrial suburb housed the Atherton Mill, a machine shop and foundry owned by Tompkins, and the Park Elevator factory. Around the factories was a neighborhood of modest dwellings for the families of workers.

By 1901, ten years after its founding, Dilworth flourished with thousands of residents and continued to grow through 1915. Almost two hundred homes built before World War I still stand today along tree-shaded avenues, and their architectual styles reflect the aspirations of the prewar suburban middle class. The Queen Anne fashion popular in Dilworth was ornate and full of gaiety, with gables and steep roofs, curving bay windows and wooden balconies, turreted cupolas and sunburst motifs. "Effete prettiness" to critics, it was

House on East Boulevard, Dilworth. Photograph by Ruth Little-Stokes. N.C. State Archives.

In 1912 Myers Park, Charlotte, Mecklenburg County, was planned as another trolley-line suburb. Wide boulevards and tree-lined winding streets, with low-lying areas reserved as parkland, made it aesthetically pleasing. Telephone and electric wires were confined to rear lot lines and commercial services were unobtrusively provided. Elizabeth College formed the gateway to the development and Presbyterian College (now Queens) was its centerpiece.

Trinity Park, Durham, was a college-centered development too. Begun in the 1890s, it was laid out in a grid pattern with its utility lines run in back alleys between the streets. Formed from Brodie Duke's estate, it provided a housing area adjacent to Trinity College (now Duke University).

"Sweetness and Light" to its admirers. Part of the "sweetness" of the Queen Anne home came from its unembarrassed delight in delicate beauty; part came from the commodious space it provided for a rich family life. A sense of enlightenment characterized both the interiors of such dwellings and their inhabitants. The furnishings were crafts and objects from all periods of history and all portions of the globe, and the residents regarded themselves as easygoing and inquisitive, a generation beyond the brash single-mindedness of those who had forged a New South.

The southern suburb of Dilworth in the early twentieth century, then, was spacious and comfortable, affordable to the middle class, and as communal or private as its residents wished it to be. A financial bonanza for developers, it became a residential sanctuary for rising social classes, a world promoted and designed to screen out the hubbub of the city and to recreate—in idyllic parks and grassy lawns—the wholesomeness of the countryside.

Manor with a Mission

In its heyday the country estate of R. J. Reynolds and his wife, Katherine Smith Reynolds, had everything that whim could wish for and money could buy. Reynolda House, open to the public since 1964 as a showcase of American paintings and a learning center for the arts, was in 1917 the centerpiece of a domain of a thousand acres. Nestled in farmland that was a long and winding two miles from downtown Winston-Salem, the country place had polo fields, a nine-hole golf course, a pure-water swimming pool, a formal English garden, a cutting garden and a greenhouse, a life-sized doll house for the two Reynolds girls, and a log cabin for the two boys. The main dwelling itself had sixty rooms, furnished with sumptuous elegance then and now. In the 1930s the family would add a bowling alley, game room, shooting gallery, enclosed swimming pool, and eight-room guest wing. For almost a half century, Reynolda served its owners and their guests as an oasis of splendor and a recreational paradise.

Yet the design of the manor house and the work carried on at the estate revealed that Reynolda was meant to be more than a palatial retreat for Winston's richest family. The Reynolds home avoided the dramatic asymmetry, endless adornment, and fortresslike immensity of other country mansions of its day. Long, lean, and low, devoid of exterior ornamentation, constructed with "thousands of loads of rock" gathered from nearby fields rather than imported from afar, Reynolda House was built in a deliberately subdued architectural fashion known as the "Bungalow" style. As one contemporary described it, this type of house "looks as if it had been built for less money than it actually cost." The design of the numerous dependency

R. J. Reynolds as a young man. Courtesy Reynolda House, Museum of American Art.

Another elegant house open to the public is the Executive Mansion, Raleigh, Wake County. Built by convict labor, 1885–91 and still staffed by prisoners, it is a triumphant example of the Queen Anne style with Eastlake decoration.

buildings mirrored the restraint of the manor, though there was no masking the reality that it took a small village of people to run the estate. Reynolda Village was a world within itself, housing living quarters for twenty families, black and white schools for their children, a church and post office, as well as barns and stables, an icehouse and smokehouse, a laundry and blacksmith shop, a power plant and telephone system. But the village was designed to serve more than the pleasure of its patrons. Reynolda was planned as a working "model farm," which would demonstrate to neighbors and those throughout the region the latest methods of scientific agriculture, particularly in the raising of livestock and dairy cattle.

Reynolda in 1917, then, was a manor with a mission. But why build such a manor and why endow it with a mission?

Like other tobacco magnates and men of wealth who made their fortunes through the industrialization of the New South, R. J. Reynolds lived in town during the nineteenth century. His home was not

Reynolda Gardens were the result of three influences. L. L. Miller, the initial landscape gardener, contributed the formal parterres along with the total plan of the estate. Thomas W. Sears added the plain garden structures of indigenous building materials in an English setting. But the dominant plantings were Mrs. Reynolds's choice: Japanese cedars, weeping cherries, and London planes.

far removed from his factory and from the employees who labored on his behalf. Of course, no one would have confused Reynolds's sprawling stone residence, with its seven-stall stable that housed the horses he regularly raced about town, for the four-room wooden dwelling of a tobacco worker. Nonetheless, as the astute Charlotte journalist Wilbur J. Cash observed, the very proximity of Reynolds and others of wealth to fellow townsmen of the working and middle classes lent an easygoing sense of familiarity to southern communities.

But in the first two decades of the twentieth century not only Reynolds but also upper-class southerners generally began to abandon the center of the city. As Cash saw it, their departure marked the moment of a widening social gulf among distant classes. Some moved to exclusive suburbs, such as Myers Park in Charlotte, where winding roads, carefully designed landscapes, and an elegant club set off the rich from the rest of society. Others opted for the more solitary splendor of a country estate. No immigrant "invasion" or mas-

Dairy barn on the farm at Reynolda. Courtesy Reynolda House, Museum of American Art.

sive urban congestion spurred the flight of southern elites to exclusive enclaves, as had happened earlier in the North. Nor was it clear that the rich felt crowded by the ambitious and successful among the middle classes, as had the abrasive New York financier J. P. Morgan, who in discussing his yacht club declared that "one could do business with anyone, but only sail with a gentleman." But the northern nouveaux riches had established the fashion of the day, and the coming of automobiles had made residences far from town accessible. All it took was the wealth to afford both—and New South fortunes were redoubling by the turn of the century.

Reynolds in particular had struck it rich, once in the nineteenth century and again in the twentieth. He had never exactly been poor, of course. Though legend had it that Dick Reynolds was an unlettered lad from Critz, Virginia, who had arrived in Winston on the back of a wagon, barefoot and dead broke, he was never a poor country boy. His father was a well-to-do planter and tobacco manufacturer with a homestead just over the Carolina-Virginia border. Reynolds had trained at college, gone to business school in Baltimore, and then acquired shrewdness and experience as a "drummer" scrambling from store to country store to sell his father's tobacco. It was not empty-handed but with $7,500 in his pocket that he struck out in 1874 for Winston, a town of 400 with a new railroad line. Over the next four decades, his first small downtown building multiplied to over 100, his work force grew to 10,000, and his $7,500 became millions. Reynolds built his nineteenth-century fortune through salesmanship and saccharin. His salesmen swarmed everywhere with their posters and calendars, "as thick as bees in a clover field." And Reynolds made his plug tobacco the "sad man's cordial" by treating it secretly with saccharin, while informing his customers that the bright leaf that grew around Winston was uniquely and "naturally sweet."

Reynolds redoubled his wealth between 1907 and 1914. Even though legally subservient from 1899 to 1911 to the American Tobacco Trust, which he had been forced to join, Reynolds refused to play lackey to James B. Duke, head of the trust. Anticipating an increase in the demand for smoking tobacco, Reynolds in 1907 introduced "Prince Albert" and hired the nation's leading advertising agency to promote the "New pipe-Joy" that "can't bite your tongue." Much to the aggravation of the trust (which at one point considered legal action), Prince Albert production soared in four years from 250,000 pounds to 14 million. After the U.S. Supreme Court declared the American Tobacco monopoly illegal in 1911, Reynolds sought supremacy in the cigarette business and won it with a rich-tasting blend of burley, bright, and Turkish leaves called Camel. Reynolds's advertising agency, with a quarter-million-dollar budget in 1914 to introduce the new cigarette, saturated the country with ads: "The Camels are Coming!" The Camels conquered. The company sold 425 million the first year and 15 billion by 1920—more than half the cigarettes smoked in the United States.

It was perhaps no surprise, as the fortunes of Reynolds and other entrepreneurs grew in the early twentieth century, that they saw in a suburban residence the chance to live with more grandeur and seclusion than in the city. Yet, though the building of a country mansion was all but assured by Reynolds's social position, the initiative and design for the estate belonged to his wife, Mary Katherine Smith Reynolds. It was Katherine Smith Reynolds who initially purchased the farmland west of downtown Winston in 1909, who commissioned the landscape and architectural plans in 1914, and who hand-initialed her final approval of the blueprints of the buildings completed in 1917. It was "K. S. Reynolds, Owner," whose name was listed formally on the business stationery of the estate. Above all, it was Reynolds's wife who decided from the outset that "Reynolda"—the Latin feminine of Reynolds—would be a "working farm," run both as a business and as a model of modern agricultural methods for the education of farmers of the Piedmont.

A country estate that attempted to blend beauty, business enterprise, and educational uplift—it was a fascinating and ambitious vision. But then Katherine Smith Reynolds, like many of her generation, was a fascinating and ambitious woman. Katherine Smith was twenty-five years old in 1905 when she wed R. J. Reynolds. He was fifty-four. They were distant cousins, and the millionaire bachelor had known her since her childhood. She had come to work for Reynolds in 1904 as his executive secretary, despite the fact that he usually relied on male secretaries. She proved trustworthy, attractive, and astute—a woman he could marry without fear that she simply wanted his wealth, a woman whose competence at business brought him a shrewd adviser, a woman whose progressive social conscience soon influenced the policies of the company and ultimately shaped the purpose of the Reynolda country estate.

Born in 1880, Katherine Smith came of age at a time when the aspirations of young middle-class women were widening dramatically. Only a handful of women born in 1850, Reynolds's own generation, had dared go to college. Higher education and ambition were thought to be ruinous to the health of the gentler sex and incompatible with the self-submergence required by family life. Katherine Smith was among the increasing minority of young girls who elected to go to college at the end of the nineteenth century. She attended in 1899 North Carolina's only state-run college for women—the State Normal and Industrial School at Greensboro (later the Woman's College of the University of North Carolina)—and finished at Sullins College, in Virginia. At Greensboro she was exposed to women faculty who were graduates of Bryn Mawr, Wellesley, and the women's medical colleges of Philadelphia and New York. The *College Yearbook* of

Katherine Smith Reynolds as a young woman. Courtesy Reynolda House, Museum of American Art.

The legislature established the State Normal and Industrial School in 1891 and made Charles D. McIver, a staunch believer in higher education for women, its first president. This college (now coeducational and part of the state system) and others like it became incubators for leaders of the women's suffrage movement in the second decade of this century. They had the support of many prominent men, such as Walter Clark, chief justice of North Carolina. He argued that because women owned one-third the property in the state, had on the average more schooling than men, and were neither mentally nor morally incompetent (bars to the ballot for men), they were being denied their constitutional rights. But North Carolina never passed a women's suffrage law and did not ratify the Nineteenth Amendment until the 1970s.

1902 reported that, while many girls began school "undeveloped in brain and soul," they gradually learned that "nothing was impossible." Greensboro students left college "with a new and hitherto unknown responsibility for the world in general" and for the "care of the lower classes" in particular.

But women's colleges taught more than paternalism. At Greensboro and elsewhere they taught skills—teaching, stenography, accounting, nutrition—and conveyed an underlying message that women should "know something and be something." At Greensboro "business ability" was especially exalted. As graduates put it in 1902, they realized at college the "necessity of becoming efficient in some line of work." A "busy woman is generally useful and those who lead 'strenuous' lives are usually happy."

A product of college and the broadened views of her age, Katherine Smith Reynolds—as her husband's business adviser and as Reynolda's director—worked on the assumption that what was humanitarian was also good business. She concerned herself especially with the welfare of those whose lives had been uprooted and dislocated by the economic transformation of the South. For the workers in her husband's factories, she persuaded her husband to open a cafeteria that offered nutritious food at low cost and a nursery for the care and early education of workers' children. A founder of the Junior League of Winston-Salem, she took a leading role in mobilizing wealthy women and the community at large behind the creation of a YWCA, a halfway house to ease the transition of country girls to urban life. When her attention turned to her country estate, she discovered that many local builders did not know how to read blueprints. She set up a school on the spot, where they learned. Once the farm was in operation, she invited neighboring farmers to view demonstrations of the latest agricultural techniques and employed students from the state agricultural college as apprentices. Riding through Reynolda Village on her horse, Kentucky Belle—she always rode astride, never sidesaddle—she gave "prizes for the best flower garden and the best-kept yard." Firmly committed to the education of the children on the estate, she attended regularly the closing programs of black and white schools.

Contemporaries of Katherine Smith Reynolds in North Carolina and elsewhere would not always find it possible to combine beauty and business, welfare and wealth. The concern of other women for the well-being of workers and the fate of farmers more than once led them on a collision course with the state's business leaders over issues of child labor, factory hours, and rural poverty. But, for the wife of R. J. Reynolds and the founder of the Reynolda farm, no such conflict emerged between what was progressive and what was profitable. The Reynolda estate—millionaire's rural retreat, model farm—married the best of both worlds.

Mrs. Reynolds and her oldest son, Dick. Courtesy Reynolda House, Museum of American Art.

A postcard with ironic comment shows
prisoners leased to the Western Railroad, 1915. N.C. State Archives.
Striped uniforms made convicts easily
identifiable.

From Jubilee to Jim Crow

The Color Line

During the Great Depression of the 1930s a farsighted employment program—the Federal Writers' Project—produced an extraordinary set of documents. Dozens of writers in North Carolina and hundreds throughout the South and the nation were hired to interview ex-slaves and to gather their recollections of life in slavery and freedom. Many aged blacks from North Carolina, looking back on six decades as free men and women, felt that emancipation had proved to be a cruel hoax. After slavery there was no more master's lash, conceded one woman, but there was also "nothin' to live on." Slavery and freedom were like two snakes, each full of poison: "Both bit de nigger and dey wus both bad." Hard work was the rule in slavery, recalled another ex-slave, and unrelieved toil remained the rule after 1865. "It's not what I has done, but what I ain't. Plowed, dug stumps, chopped, broke steers, ginned cotton, cooked for white folks." One Johnston County man admitted to being an ambitious "high-minded younger nigger"—but something always undercut him. Cheated on his crop by a warehouseman, he "went crazy," hit him, got "twelve months on the road," and learned his lesson: "no use for me to try to ever make anything but just a living."

Were these recollections from the depths of the depression too pessimistic? Possibly. Yet it was beyond question that hard-won freedoms gained in the first three decades after emancipation had come under savage assault at the end of the 1890s and stood gutted by 1920. State constitutional amendments and the all-white party primary had eliminated the right to vote for all but a few blacks after 1900—a far cry from 1896, when 87 percent of the eligible black voters cast their ballots. Black jurymen, officeholders, and constables, numerous in the eighties and nineties, vanished from public life. Only three in ten black farmers in 1920 owned their own land, and their soil was often the most marginal, the "back bone and the spare ribs." The overwhelming majority of rural black families remained share-croppers or tenants, and for many "settling up" time was reminiscent of slavery: "Naught is naught and figger is a figger, all for de white man and none for de nigger."

Many former slaves had left the plantations and migrated to towns and cities "to find out if I wuz really free." And until 1900 the state's urban centers had indeed proved to be "Black Meccas." Though most black city dwellers were unskilled laborers and domes-

Crew of Tar River steamer, ca. 1900.
N.C. State Archives.

Potter. Photograph by Margaret Morley.
N.C. State Archives.

tics, fully half the skilled workers of North Carolina's cities in 1900 were black. They were stevedores and printers in Wilmington, barbers and brickmakers in Durham, masons and carpenters in Greensboro and Winston. Those gains, too, were destroyed by law and custom after 1900, as white employers, lawmakers, and working people segregated the city's skilled jobs and restricted them to whites only.

A Durham woman recalled vividly the imposition of segregation early in the twentieth century and its endless humiliations. Pauli Murray grew up in the "bottoms" of Durham. The marshy lowland was typical of the portion of North Carolina towns reserved for most blacks: a hollow full of "washed out gullies," "shacks for factory workers," "trash piles, garbage dumps, cow stalls, pigpens, and crowded humanity." In the 1890s her grandfather had built his two-story wooden house toward the base of a steep hill with a wheat field on it, but by 1900 "the town had moved in upon us" and the sprawling town cemetery "had swallowed the wheatfield."

But it was not her grandfather's loss of his land to the all-white cemetery that festered in Pauli Murray's memory. In her moving autobiography, *Proud Shoes*, she tells of "the signs which literally screamed at me from every side—on streetcars, over drinking fountains, on doorways: FOR WHITE ONLY, FOR COLORED ONLY, WHITE LADIES, COLORED WOMEN, WHITE, COLORED. If I missed the signs I had only to follow my nose to the dirtiest, smelliest, most neglected accommodations." Each morning on her way to school, she "passed white children as poor as I going in the opposite direction. . . . We never had fights; I don't recall their ever having called me a single insulting name. It was worse than that. They passed me as if I weren't there!" The whites' school was a "beautiful red-and-white brick building," its "lawn was large and green and watered every day," their "playground was a wonderland of iron swings, sand slides, seesaws"—always "barred from us by a strong eight-foot-high fence topped by barbed wire." Her own school was dilapidated and rickety, a two-story wooden building that "creaked and swayed in the wind as if it might collapse." Inside, the "floors were bare and splintery, the plumbing was leaky, and the toilets in the basement smelly and constantly out of order."

For Pauli Murray the hurt of segregation was "never the hardship so much as the *contrast* between what we had and what the white children had. We got the greasy, torn, dog-eared books; they got the new ones. They got wide mention in the newspaper; we got a paragraph at the bottom." In Durham, as in every other town in the region, the blacks "were bottled up and labeled and set aside—sent to the Jim Crow car, the back of the bus, the side door of the theater, the side window of a restaurant." Black children soon "came to understand that no matter how neat and clean, how law-abiding, submissive and polite, how studious at school, how churchgoing and moral, how scrupulous in paying our bills and taxes we were, it made no essential difference in our place." It seemed as if "there were only two kinds of people in the world—*They* and *We*—*White* and *Colored.*"

Like many black North Carolinians thwarted and wearied by segregation, Pauli Murray left the Tar Heel state for the North. Her attainments in exile were remarkable. She became a civil rights field-worker and spokesman, a distinguished lawyer, a poet and writer, and in 1977 the first Negro woman ordained a priest in the history of the Protestant Episcopal church.

Clearly, Pauli Murray flourished in response to opportunities away from home. Yet she also built upon a long North Carolina heritage of black accomplishment and striving. She built on the achievements of those who opened the first schools for black youths and adults after 1865 and who "taught not merely to impart knowledge but to build character and shape the future." She built on the philosophy of uplift and black self-help—of "dogged work and manly striving"—that had taken root in nearly a dozen black colleges founded in the state after the war. She built on the special heritage of Durham, where the values of self-help and racial solidarity were funneled into business enterprise. The "grit and greenback" of Durham's blacks had produced "the Negro Wall Street of America," a downtown block dotted with black businesses and dominated after 1921 by the six-

North Carolina Mutual and Provident Association, ca. 1910. Courtesy North Carolina Mutual Life Insurance Company. Along this block of Parrish Street, Durham, were a number of black financial institutions that accounted for its nickname, "the Negro Wall Street."

Office of the North Carolina Mutual and Provident Association, early 1900s, with John Merrick, C. C. Spaulding, and Dr. A. M. Moore. Courtesy North Carolina Mutual Life Insurance Company.

story skyscraper of the North Carolina Mutual Life Insurance Company. Above all, Pauli Murray built her life of commitment to racial liberation upon a southern black heritage of spiritual strength and political struggle. That striving for independence surged to the surface in the Year of Jubilee and found expression in all-black churches and all-black conventions that the new freedmen organized after 1865.

Independence Halls

The Emancipation Proclamation of 1863 and the Thirteenth Amendment to the Constitution in 1865 forever ended slavery in the United States. But the legal actions simply set the stage for a more fundamental struggle. What did freedom mean?

Many of the historic places where that battle was contested in North Carolina are gone. Gone is the Union army campsite of occupied New Bern in 1864, where the sight of "hundreds of colored soldiers armed" and ready to fight for their own emancipation overwhelmed a black sergeant: "I can only say, the fetters have fallen—our bondage is over." Gone is the Front Street Methodist Church of Wilmington, where for the better part of 1865 black members of the congregation struggled for control of the sanctuary. A mood of jubilation and independence among hundreds of black church members was evident at the first sunrise prayer meeting after the occupation of the city in January 1865. "The whole congregation was wild with excitement," recalled the white minister; the meeting was "extravagant beyond all precedent with shouts, groans, amens." After hymns and prayers, the black class leader chose the Ninth Psalm for the day of jubilee and "read as only Charles could read." As he said: "I will sing praise to thy name, O thou most High. When mine enemies are turned back, they shall fall and perish at thy presence. . . . For the needy shall not always be forgotten: the expectation of the poor shall *not* perish for ever. Arise, O LORD." Then a black army chaplain, who a few years before had "left North Carolina a slave," strode to the pulpit. "One week ago you were all slaves; now you are all free. (Uproarious screamings!) Thank God the armies of the Lord and of Gideon has triumphed. . . . (Amen! Hallelujah!)"

Black members fought for nine months to affiliate the congregation with the African Methodist Episcopal (A.M.E.) church—and in the meantime repeatedly came down from the balcony to sit in the body of the church. They finally withdrew and helped form the St. Stephen A.M.E. Church, whose sanctuary built in 1880 still stands on Fifth Street in Wilmington.

St. Stephen A.M.E. Church, Wilmington, New Hanover County, built in 1880. This structure replaced an earlier wooden building from the late 1860s when the congregation was formed by Negroes who withdrew from the Front Street Methodist Church and affiliated with the African Methodist Episcopal church.

St. Paul A.M.E. Zion Church, at Edenton and Harrington streets, Raleigh, is a descendant of this early congregation.

James Hood (1831–1918). N.C. State Archives.

Were it still standing today, the two-story wooden building of the A.M.E. Church in Raleigh might be regarded as the Independence Hall of black North Carolinians. In this modest structure, located on a back street just a few blocks from the old State Capitol, black delegates from all over the state declared themselves a "Convention of Freedmen" on 29 September 1865. The 115 men, most slaves just months before, met to find ways to eradicate the legal inequities of the past. They timed their convention to coincide with the assembly of whites who convened blocks away in the state legislative chamber to form a new civil government. For four days they deliberated in the sparsely furnished church, its floor and gallery filled to its capacity of four hundred by delegates, spectators, and reporters. Ever on view behind the pulpit was a lifelike bust of Abraham Lincoln, shrouded in mourning, with the inscription overhead: "With malice toward none, with charity for all, with firmness in the right."

Appointed to draw up a set of resolves to address the white Constitutional Convention, the delegates debated heatedly the issue of charity and firmness. What rights should they seek? Should they request or demand? Alexander Galloway, a former North Carolina slave who had escaped to Ohio in 1857 and become an abolitionist, favored immediate and universal suffrage. In "six months," he contended, white leaders "would be putting their arms around our necks and begging" for black votes. But James Harris, another North Carolinian, advocated reliance on the goodwill of the "intelligent white class of the South." Freed from slavery in 1850, Harris had traveled to Africa and the West Indies—"40,000 miles in search of a better country"—and concluded that the freedman's place was on his home soil. Though he believed unequivocally in the right of blacks to testify in court, to serve on juries, and to vote, he advocated for the moment a "patient and respectful demeanor" to win white confidence. Proving themselves worthy, blacks would "receive what they had a right to claim."

Ironically, it was a northern-born, free black minister, an indomitable leader who spent the rest of his life building the African Methodist Episcopal Zion church in North Carolina and the South, who presided over the convention and successfully urged it to strike a tone of moderation. James Hood, born in Pennsylvania and formerly a minister in Connecticut, exhorted the delegates to refrain from "harsh language." "We and the white people have to live here together." The best way was "to treat all men respectfully. Respectability will always gain respect." The final address avoided mention of juries and suffrage and appealed to the "moral consciences" of whites. In return for black "industry, sobriety, and moral demeanor," the conciliatory address requested that whites pay blacks properly for their labor, educate their children, and repeal "oppressive laws." "Is this asking too much?"

74

It was. Meeting less than a year later in the same Raleigh A.M.E. Church, black delegates denounced the "killing, shooting, and robbing" of "unprotected people" that had characterized the intervening months. They no longer looked to the state legislature for a redress of grievances but to the North and the national Congress. By 1867, under federal edict, black North Carolinians were voting and serving on juries. In January 1868, when a second convention met in the capitol to draft a new constitution and government, fifteen blacks—including the three leaders from the first freedmen's assembly—took their seats alongside whites as duly elected delegates.

While churches were often sources of political initiative, they served more fundamentally as vibrant centers of spiritual vitality and communal life. Whether they worshiped in brush-arbors built out of branches and leaves, or in wooden buildings such as the Raleigh A.M.E. Church, or in handsome brick structures such as St. Stephen, it was in sanctuaries they built themselves that black North Carolinians felt most free. The release from bondage offered the chance to serve the Lord without white surveillance or opposition, to plumb the meaning of the Scripture without outside guidance or rebuke, to express the love of Jesus without encumbrance of white notions of restraint.

Colleges for Uplift

The difficulties encountered by blacks of North Carolina in their political struggles highlighted the reality that their path to independence was to be different from the paths more familiar to white Americans. There was no bounteous Promised Land for them to flee to, where they could escape oppression and start afresh. There was no immortal declaration of their right to life, liberty, and the pursuit of happiness—indeed, most whites in 1865 questioned whether the inalienable rights of man belonged to blacks. Nor was it clear that the nineteenth-century road to freedom—ascent through hard work and the assimilation of middle-class cultural traits—would be available to blacks. Even after freedmen made "earnest efforts by education, virtue, industry, and economy to qualify ourselves for the highest stations in life"—as New Bern ex-slaves pledged themselves to do in 1865—there was no guarantee that whites would open higher stations to worthy blacks.

The philosophy of uplift and a commitment to black self-help took firm root in nearly a dozen black colleges founded in North Carolina after the war. Handsome buildings named for out-of-state benefactors still grace the campuses of Shaw University in Raleigh, Johnson C. Smith University in Charlotte, and Livingstone College in Salisbury. Each of the schools started in small frame or log buildings,

Charles N. Hunter, black Raleigh educator and journalist, saw that blacks would have to win their place in society: "We don't seem to realize the fact, that to occupy a respectable position among other nations of the world, we must make corresponding advances in literature, the sciences, arts, and everything else having a tendency to elevate and ennoble us. That we must sustain colored papers, Doctors and Lawyers; that we must produce historians and men,—and women, too—for be it known that your correspondent is an humble advocate of the rights of women,—of every honorable calling." Charles N. Hunter Papers.

Martin Tupper (1831–93). Morehouse, *H. M. Tupper, D. D.*

Carnegie Library, 1911, at Biddle University, now Johnson C. Smith University, Charlotte, Mecklenburg County, was one of ten built with Carnegie money in North Carolina. A northern philanthropist, Carnegie by his gifts of hundreds of libraries throughout the nation provided the greatest single incentive to library growth.

and each began with the mission of training young people to become "Christian workers" and educated ministers who could combat the "spirit preachers" of the day.

Two of the schools received their only early support from northern churches and the Freedmen's Bureau and faced serious opposition from native whites. The Reverend Henry Martin Tupper, the Massachusetts Baptist minister who founded Shaw in Raleigh, was threatened by the Ku Klux Klan in the 1860s. Continuing tension and ostracism in the mid-1870s produced teachers who were, in the eyes of one outside observer, the "most forbidding New England type— with whom duty—in all matters—is always a business and never a pleasure." Yet, "the truth is that a less cold & determined set of people would be badgered almost to death & driven away." The first years of the "Freedman's College" in Charlotte—which would become the Biddle Memorial Institute and finally Johnson C. Smith University—were no less trying for the native white ministers who founded the Presbyterian school in 1865. Fellow churchmen forced the ministers to disaffiliate themselves and the school from the southern church. By the time the African Methodist Episcopal church established Livingstone College in Salisbury in the 1880s, however, white North Carolinians saw the merit of colleges designed to educate the clergy and instruct black youths in both the liberal arts and industrial skills.

Each of the colleges established early a close relationship with northern patrons who nurtured and sustained the schools well into the twentieth century. Estey Hall at Shaw, a handsome dormitory for girls that made possible the "Christian education" of women at the Baptist college, was funded in 1870 by a family from Vermont. The striking administration building at Johnson C. Smith University as well as the school's dormitories, Science Hall, and Carnegie Library were the products of northern benefactions and set the stage for the bequest in 1924 from James B. Duke of a 4 percent annual increment from the forty-million-dollar Duke Endowment. Contributions from British donors helped to establish Livingstone College, Rowan County. Named after the famous British missionary David Livingstone, the college pledged itself to support Livingstone's work by training "intelligent, moral, and well prepared men, to preach the gospel of Christ" and "elevate their brethren in Africa." The names of buildings on the Livingstone campus—Dodge Hall, Stanford Seminary, Carnegie Library—testify to the continuing interest of philanthropists from the North and West.

From the 1890s onward, the black colleges and the first generation of graduates faced a time of testing. Black faculty and administrators replaced the predominantly white staffs of the colleges in Raleigh and Charlotte—and performed ably despite the anxieties of some white trustees that blacks were not yet ready for command. Indus-

Estey Hall, Shaw University, Raleigh, built in 1874. N.C. State Archives. Jacob Estey and Sons, of Brattleboro, Vermont, gave the money for this dormitory for girls.

James Edward Shepard, a native of Raleigh and graduate of Shaw, started the National Training School and Chautauqua in 1910; this became North Carolina College, now North Carolina Central University, Durham, the first state-supported liberal arts college for blacks in the United States.

trial education, favored by some blacks and many whites as the most practical curriculum for black youths, challenged but did not displace the teaching of the liberal arts and the preparation of increasing numbers of students for the professions. But for those students whom the colleges did train for "higher stations" there was frustration. Some graduates went on to become lawyers and physicians, teachers and ministers, but others made their living as porters and chauffeurs and waiters. Many were resented for their achievements, condemned for their aspirations, and commanded to remain second-class citizens in an era that saw the triumph of segregation.

After no small struggle in the 1890s, black graduates found themselves obliged to "make the best of segregation" as the twentieth century began. The choice by 1920 was "between taking segregation standing up and taking it lying down." Until the day when the struggle for an integrated society could be resumed, a commencement speaker advised graduates to concentrate on building black "institutions so that they are as good as anyone else's institutions" and in the meantime repel "spiritual defeat." Their credo should be: "I will not allow one prejudiced person or one million or one hundred million to blight my life. My inner life is mine, and I shall defend and maintain its integrity against all the powers of Hell." In the protracted era of Jim Crow, the mission of the black college was to provide each student with a "solid belief in his own race, a zeal to serve his own people, a spirit of dignity, and a courageous style of life."

Redemption would come in the 1960s. North Carolina's black college students, seating themselves at segregated lunch counters first in Greensboro and then throughout the state, spearheaded the successful struggle against segregation in public accommodations throughout the South. Within weeks of the first sit-in, hundreds met at Shaw University to form the Student Non-Violent Coordinating Committee, which soon funneled the energies of thousands of educated young men and women into the swelling crusade for civil rights. What happened at Greensboro and what happened at Shaw surely would have pleased those who had dedicated a century of effort to educational uplift, racial self-help, and a "courageous style of life."

Black Business and White Supremacy

The North Carolina Mutual Life Insurance Company Building, which dominates the south side of Parrish Street in downtown Durham—and its gleaming twelve-story successor, a daring architectural pillar of glass and concrete built on the hill that once accommodated the estate of the son of Washington Duke—stand as testimony to black achievement amidst adversity. A thousand guests attended the dedication of the Parrish Street office structure in 1921 and celebrated the opening of the building as a monument to "Negro progress." To the keynote speaker, the new Mutual home—with its neoclassical design, marble trim, and solid metallic doors—symbolized the "industrial prowess of our group [and] our potentialities as a race." The speaker saw the edifice as a clear message to North Carolina blacks about how to make the most of forced segregation. "Let us put our money in Negro banks, read Negro newspapers, trade in Negro stores, patronize Negro doctors, employ Negro lawyers, carry life insurance with Negro companies." "The white man builds businesses for the employment of white boys and girls; we must build businesses for the employment of black boys and girls." Whites, too, applauded the "architectural gem . . . of white brick rising above all other buildings on Parrish Street"—the height had been carefully chosen so as not to exceed the tallest white-owned skyscraper in Durham. The Mutual building, editorialized the *Durham Morning Herald*, was "an example of what can be done by the negro if he goes about it in the right way."

North Carolina Mutual Life Insurance Company, built in 1921. Courtesy of the company.

Drugstore in the Young Men's Institute (YMI), Asheville, Buncombe County, ca. 1910. N.C. State Archives. George Vanderbilt constructed this building to serve the social, educational, and religious needs of blacks in Asheville.

To a black Durham tobacco worker, the Mutual Building and the black Mechanics and Farmers Bank housed on its first floor were more than symbols. A Mutual insurance policy provided a measure of family protection, and the black bank offered the enterprising man a way to get ahead. "Back in those times, a Negro was frowned on in a bank when you're talking about a loan unless you had some powerful white man to sanction it. You couldn't get nothing on your merit." With a black-operated bank, "you could underwrite a whole lot of stuff." "They set up the bank right downtown—not in the black community—but in the heart of town. That gave Negroes a push-off."

In the broadest sense, the Mutual was descended from a century-old tradition of black fraternal and burial societies, built around the ideas of self-help and moral improvement and organized to provide sickness and burial insurance. With the end of Reconstruction and the waning of the quest for black advancement through civil rights and integration, black self-help and benefit societies mushroomed. Many, like the Grand United Order of the True Reformers, provided ritual and regalia, recreation and recognition, in addition to the promise of "happiness, peace, plenty, thrift, and protection" through insurance. But few black benefit societies of the 1860s made hardnosed appraisals of the mortality prospects of their members. Those companies founded in the 1890s, like the Mutual, were the first to offer health and life policies on a businesslike basis. Yet the Mutual was always more than a company dedicated to making insurance pay, a black imitation of the "triumphant commercialism" of the "conquering Anglo-Saxons." It remained also committed to the uplift of the unfortunate and the good of the black community, a company—as its slogan stated—"with A Soul and a Service."

The founding of the Mutual was a by-product as well of the special circumstances of Durham, a booming industrial city of the New South that boasted that it had "no aristocracy but the aristocracy of labor." Within limits, Durham's white businessmen encouraged black enterprise, provided occasional capital to black entrepreneurs, and sanctioned the aspirations of Durham's blacks to be successful men. Washington Duke spoke for many when he told the city's black leaders in 1890 that "a proper ambition is God's call to a higher life." Zeal for Durham as a special seedbed for black capitalism was shared by the town's first Negro newspaper: "Everything here is push, everything is on the move, every citizen is looking out for everything that will make Durham great. The Negro in the midst of such life has caught the disease and . . . has awakened to action. Durham! The very name has become a synonymous term for energy, pluck, and business ability." White contributions to black philanthropies and churches furthered the reputation of the city as an oasis of racial harmony. The interior of St. Joseph's A.M.E. Church in Durham, a spacious and beautiful brick sanctuary built in 1892, testifies to the unusual relationship of Durham's black and white elites. Across from the oval stained glass window of Jesus Christ is a window of equal size portraying Washington Duke.

Yet, in a fundamental way, the Mutual was founded in response to the reign of terror visited upon North Carolina's blacks during the successful white-supremacy campaign of the 1890s. It was in October of 1898, the first year of the terror, that John Merrick of Durham—a black entrepreneur who owned three white and three black barbershops and who served as the personal barber to Washington Duke—gathered together six other men in skilled trades and professions to lay the basis for the company. In the red-shirted vigilantes who broke up black political rallies and threatened violence to blacks who came to the polls, in the gruesome lynching of a black man

From its birth as a brush arbor in 1869, the first organized church within the corporate limits of Durham, St. Joseph's A.M.E. Church, has become the leading congregation of this denomination in the state. Its first minister, the Reverend Edian Markham, had been born a slave in 1824 and had escaped bondage by the Underground Railroad. He educated himself in New York and then chose Durham as his first missionary field. The congregation he formed was first called Union Bethel.

between Durham and Chapel Hill, they each had seen the handwriting on the wall. Though five of the Mutual's founders had been active in the Republican party, they concluded that October evening that they must abandon politics and the assertion of their rights. Blacks must instead turn to "education, business and industrial progress," "keep quiet and saw wood," and turn their "attention to making money." In "commercial opportunity" they would "hammer away. The almighty dollar is the magic wand that knocks the bottom out of race prejudice and all the humbugs that fatten on it."

If the Mutual's seven founders needed reinforcement for their decision to withdraw from politics in favor of white-approved business pursuits, it came within a month. Two days after the November 1898 elections, which saw the triumph of a brutal campaign to restore white supremacy to the state, the white leaders of Wilmington authorized and led an attack on the blacks of that city. They unleashed a rampage of white retaliation for years of black striving and political success.

Regarded by its Negro majority as a "Black Mecca," Wilmington since the 1880s had pulsated with energetic black stevedores and skilled artisans, black-run cafes and confectionery shops, black lawyers and pharmacists. It had two black newspapers in the 1890s and a core of black political leaders without peer in the state. They had pressed for and received the appointment of modest numbers of blacks to civil service posts in the community. Wilmington had black policemen and firemen, a black coroner and assistant register of deeds, and a black held the important post of collector of customs in the port city.

The white elite of Wilmington decided in the autumn of 1898 to use the election campaign to put the town's blacks—and especially its educated and politically active leadership—back in their place. Throughout the fall, they charged that the black aldermen and white Republicans who constituted a majority on the city council represented "NEGRO DOMINATION!" Repeatedly, they held up to the white workingmen of the city the image of black townsmen living in luxury, with servants in their houses and pianos in their living rooms. Incessantly they reprinted and denounced the editorial of a Wilmington black newspaper that firmly denied that Negroes were rapist fiends, denounced whites as "carping hypocrites" who "cry aloud for the virtue of your women, when you seek to destroy the morality of ours," and boldly asserted that it was "well known" that many blacks "were sufficiently attractive for white girls of culture and refinement to fall in love with them."

On the morning of 10 November 1898, promising an immediate end "to these intolerable conditions" even "if we have to choke the current of the Cape Fear River with carcasses," white leaders struck. They forced the black and white Republican aldermen to resign, smashed the press of the city's black newspaper, and set fire to the building that housed the beleaguered journal. Only a photograph remains of the gutted two-story, wooden structure. The building had been the mutual society meeting place of Wilmington's black women and was ironically named the Love and Charity Hall. The photo was made immediately after the fire as a portrait of those who sacked the hall. They posed for posterity in front of the building, rifles and pistols in hand, attired for their task in coats and ties and derby hats. The attack triggered a forty-eight-hour invasion of the black community that left numbers of blacks dead and that forced hundreds to flee the city for their lives. After days in the woods and the swamps, afraid to light fires to warm themselves against the steady, bone-chilling rain, the women and children and workingmen cautiously came back to their homes. The most skilled among them would soon see their jobs taken by whites. Dozens among Wilmington's educated leaders, "banished" as "objectionable persons," never returned.

The lesson of the vendetta of 1898 was not lost on Wilmington's ministers or on Durham's black businessmen. The pastor of Wilmington's Central Baptist Church counseled "the Negro race" to "be considerate in all that they do. Conduct themselves as gentlemen and ladies, and try by all means to keep the peace that is necessary in this country." The minister of St. Luke's A.M.E. Zion Church, whose sanctuary stood next to the destroyed Love and Charity Hall, had a stern message in his sermon the Sunday after the riot: "If the Negro

Love and Charity Hall after the fire.
Collier's magazine, 26 November 1898.

Artist H. Ditzler's drawing of the Wilmington riot. *Collier's* magazine, 26 November 1898.

trusted in God and minded his own business, all would be well." For his part, John Merrick of North Carolina Mutual concluded, "The Negroes have had lots of offices in this state and they have benefitted themselves but very little. . . . Had the Negroes of Wilmington owned half of the city . . . there wouldn't anything happened to them [to] compare with what did. Let us think more of our employment and what it takes to keep peace and to build us a little house."

Out of the ashes of disaster came a rededication to self-help, racial solidarity, and to the magic wand of the "almighty dollar" that would "knock the bottom out of race prejudice."

Aerial performers in a street carnival, ca. 1900. Photograph by K. W. Parkham. N.C. State Archives.

Corn shucking at a Greene County farm, ca. 1900. Courtesy Bill Murphy.

Lucy Spencer, of Stokes County, described such an occasion: "When Papa had a corn shucking, every man for miles around came. And about four or five women would come and help cook. And, oh boy, those big old pots of chicken and dumplings! Oh, yes, they'd start in the morning. And it'd be in the wintertime when the days weren't so long. Just as soon as the sun got up a little bit, they'd get out there and start shucking. And they'd just shuck all day long. But it was fun." Ginns, *Rough Weather Makes Good Timber.*

84

The New Leisure

The Birth of Recreation

Few North Carolinians who lived in the countryside thought in 1870 of formal places or formal times for "recreation." Their pleasures were rural and often linked naturally with the outdoors and with work. Carolinians of all ages loved to fish and to hunt and savored nothing more than the aroma and satisfaction of a fire crackling under a good day's catch. Labor and leisure, music and work, flowed together easily at a typical corn shucking or quilting bee. When the workday ended and when the Sabbath came, visiting was the Carolinian's customary way to relax and the family porch was the customary place. Not all good times, of course, were homebred. Much fun was brewed up in outlaw outposts of leisure—gambling cabins, whiskey stills, makeshift cockfight arenas—that were buried in the woods and known only to a privileged few (and sometimes to the sheriff as well).

But, with the passing of time, the improvement of roads, and the growth of towns and cities, new kinds of recreational activities and settings emerged. At the county fair, farmers came and showed their animals; women arrived with pies and breads. A mix of agricultural display and carnival, the county fair was a place where one could see and smell the livestock, take the rides, perhaps visit sideshows of freaks and voluptuous shady ladies. The largest of the fairs took place in Raleigh. The traveling circus was a second attraction. Town and country folk alike enjoyed its opening parade of costumed travelers and the dazzling array of exotic animals and acrobatic feats. The physical sites themselves were as evanescent as the big top: pitched today, gone tomorrow.

In towns and cities particularly, recreational opportunities enlarged. Once the civic elite of a community felt itself secure and monied enough to take stock of its amenities, conservatories of music, opera houses for theatrical performances, and lyceum halls for lectures took their places on or near Main Street. Sometimes, as in the town of Apex, the city hall housed both the governmental offices of the community and the town's performance hall. In the first two decades of the twentieth century, the great popular medium of the movies came to town. In gala movie houses with elegant names—the Majestic, the Royal, the Orpheum—Carolina townspeople laughed and wept at the antics and passions of the wider world on film.

Parade in Forest City, Rutherford County, ca. 1915. N.C. State Archives.

"Fishing was a poor man's sport and a lazy man's recreation." Taylor, *Carolina Crossroads.*

William Tillinghast attended the 1875 state fair at a newly purchased fifty-five-acre tract on Hillsboro Street, today opposite the State college campus. "The day was beautiful & the fair quite a success. Goods from the stores fill up very much, but on the whole the display except of cookery was very good. The cookery (bread & cakes) was about 4 or 5 ft. on one shelf. There were many interesting machines which I did not have time to investigate—I saw a one horse cultivator which I thought would suit my garden & vines exactly—The flowers were very pretty. . . . The display of vegetables was excellent. . . . The Grand Stand is an *immense* building & affords room for *all* to see the races easily." Tillinghast Family Papers.

Particularly in commercial and factory cities the stress of work created the need for places of repose and release. As Carolina cities grew, there was usually a moment of recognition that the countryside that people had once taken for granted was no longer readily accessible—and that refuges for rest and diversion were more important than ever. Especially if the urban young were not to be left to places of base abandonment—saloons, brothels, gambling dens, dance halls—more civilized arenas of amusement had to be created.

Bloomsbury in Raleigh was planned as such an oasis of genteel delight. It was one of the many amusement parks designed to combine the pleasures of the country with the heightened energy of the city. The central attraction—moved to Pullen Park in 1921 and now mostly restored—was a majestic carousel. There one could ride on a carved wooden horse of bedazzling color, a knightly steed that rhythmically rose and dipped to the popular music of the day. Nearby was a dance pavilion, a penny arcade, and a roller coaster as well as landscaped grounds with picnic tables and bicycle paths. In its fascinating mix of traditional rusticity and machine-made toys, Bloomsbury restored the energy depleted by work and provided healthy diversion and controlled delights for young and old.

Carousel, Pullen Park, Raleigh, Wake County. N.C. State Archives. The merry-go-round, built by the Dentzel Carousel Company of Philadelphia (1903–9) and featuring the handcarved animals of Salvatore Cernigliaro, first stood in Bloomsbury Park. The animals, whose glass eyes were produced in Czechoslovakia, are older than those in the Smithsonian Institution.

Cover of an advertising prospectus. Duke University Library.

Resorts for the Well-to-do

Almost since the first human habitation of North Carolina, visitors have been attracted by the majesty and bounty of its unspoiled outdoors. Many came to look, lingered to visit, and stayed to settle. The pattern of discovery was repeated in the late nineteenth century, when northern city dwellers in search of health came to Carolina for its unpolluted air, tarried, and returned to savor its natural beauty. The visitors of the late nineteenth century were the energetic new rich of the Gilded Age. Their patronage not only launched the state's resort industry; by the 1890s some were using their fortunes to purchase vast tracts of land, upon which they would impose their own visions for the region's development. Three such enclaves of the new leisure class—Pinehurst, the Grove Park Inn, Biltmore and the adjacent Cradle of Forestry—were fascinating offspring of Carolina soil and outside wealth.

Health and pleasure first drew urban outsiders to the Sandhills and Appalachian Mountains of North Carolina after the Civil War. A postwar surge in tuberculosis and lung disorders led physicians and their patients to Asheville, where high altitude, pure air, and pure water were ideal for the founding of America's first sanatorium in the 1870s. Nestled amidst glorious scenery were large wooden buildings, girdled by spacious porches and abounding with rocking chairs. The setting guaranteed vast daily doses of curative fresh air. In the mid-1880s promoters from the Sandhills joined the competition for northern pleasure-seekers and invalids and sought to lure them to Southern Pines. For those who simply wanted a southern vacation it was

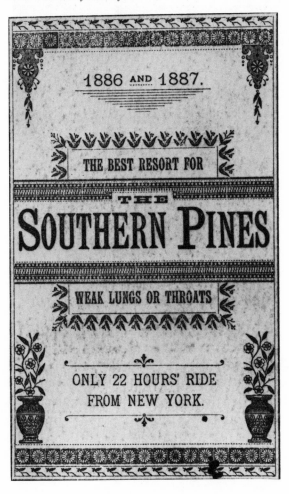

1886 AND 1887.

THE BEST RESORT FOR

THE
SOUTHERN PINES

WEAK LUNGS OR THROATS

ONLY 22 HOURS' RIDE
FROM NEW YORK.

Real estate development in the North Carolina mountains and Sandhills capitalized on the belief that pines were salutary. In the 1880s the State Board of Agriculture and Immigration subdivided a twelve-hundred-acre tract and gave away lots to attract settlement in what is today Southern Pines.

Polo players at Pinehurst. North Carolina Collection.

The health angle had been so successfully exploited, particularly attracting tuberculosis sufferers, that Tufts feared its effect on general vacationers. In his advertising brochure, he wrote: "No case of consumption nor malaria has been known to originate in the locality *and Pinehurst is the only village* in the country where consumptives are absolutely excluded." *Pinehurst, North Carolina,* North Carolina Collection.

Besides golf, tennis, and polo, Pinehurst offered its guests hunting and target-practice. In 1915 the management hired Annie Oakley, who had retired from the vaudeville and circus circuits because of ill health, to teach target-shooting at Pinehurst, where her "wild west" fame added glamour to the new resort.

"Only 22 Hours' Ride from New York." For persons with "Weak Lungs or Throats," it was the best resort "for regaining health." Not mountain air but the "health-giving and delicious odor" of the "noble pines" would restore the lungs to vigor.

Tuberculosis had prompted the choice of Asheville and Southern Pines as health resorts for the ailing. By the end of the nineteenth century, important changes in northern values galvanized their growth as vacation havens for the well. That vacations were desirable was by no means obvious to the urban middle class at mid-century. In industrializing America, debate raged over whether or not any play was fitting in a world devoted to work. For aristocrats in the North and South, of course, the cultivation of leisure and resort life had always been part of civilized life. But northerners new to wealth had to be exhorted to take a rest by a new "gospel of relaxation." Neurologists of the 1870s warned that the compulsion to *"Overwork"* led to chronic nervousness or "neurasthenia" and to its symptomatic headaches, melancholy, dyspepsia, insomnia, and spinal pains. By 1900 *Success Magazine* insisted that "Fun Is a Necessity," and the *Saturday Evening Post* dismissed an opponent of paid vacations as "an awful example of . . . industry gone mad."

Enterprising North Carolinians perceived and responded to the heightened demand for middle- and upper-class playgrounds, far away from the hyperactive urban centers. But it fell to the richest of their clients, vacationers from outside who had acquired vast fortunes in the Gilded Age, to envision and create North Carolina's most monumental enclaves of leisure.

It was James Tufts of Boston, for example, who founded Pinehurst. His fortune had come through his invention of modern soda fountain equipment that made carbonated water. The head of the American Soda Fountain Company, Tufts was sensitive to the importance of rest and healthful climes because of his own physical frailness. He also loved golf. He heard about the healthful climate of the Sandhills of North Carolina from New Englanders who had wintered there in the 1880s and early 1890s. In 1895 Tufts decided to build a resort that would bring relaxation and good health to men and women of moderate means. He bought five thousand acres of cutover timberland, built cottages and stores, graded streets and constructed a trolley line to nearby Southern Pines, built Pinehurst's first golf course in 1898, opened the Holly Inn and the grand Carolina Hotel for the accommodation of hundreds of guests. With a New Englander's penchant for planning, he hired the nation's leading landscaping firm to lay out winding roads and to supervise the planting of a quarter million plants, a fifth of them imported from France.

Two years after the beginning of Pinehurst in 1895, North Carolina's clime lured a second millionaire to the state in search of relief from ill health. E. W. Grove was delighted at the disappearance of his bronchial disorder weeks after his arrival in Asheville. But he was even more taken with the grandeur of the mountains and with the unrealized possibility of making Asheville into a resort city on a scale more colossal than any native had contemplated. Thinking on a grand scale had become second nature to Grove. A Tennessee native with a third-grade education and a self-taught pharmacist, he had accidentally discovered a method for suspending quinine in water and had gone on to found the Bromo-Quinine elixir empire with headquarters in St. Louis. To transform Asheville into a resort for the finest, the "Chill Tonic King" decided he had to end that town's career as a sanctuary for the tubercular. So he bought and burned every sanatorium in town. Simultaneously, the multimillionaire purchased thousands of acres of farmland on Asheville's northern fringe. The stage was set for the fulfillment of his vision: constructing the Grove Park Inn, "the finest resort hotel in the world."

And what a resort it was! Designed by Grove's son-in-law, who had received three months' architectural training at Princeton, it was built in 1913 by 400 laborers working round the clock for eleven

Grove Park Inn, Asheville, Buncombe County. Built in 1913 by Grove on a plan of his son-in-law, Fred Seely, Jr., the inn was fittingly dedicated by William Jennings Bryan, the famous orator, who undoubtedly approved of the literary quotations from Ovid to Emerson written on the huge boulders over the fireplace: "Every man is a quotation from all his ancestors," of Emerson; "Take things always by the smooth handle," of Jefferson; or Thoreau's "Be not simply good —be good for something."

Green Park Hotel, Blowing Rock, Watauga County.

The largest religious denominations in the state developed their own resorts to provide their members recreation with congenial company in an atmosphere of spiritual uplift. The Methodists have Lake Junaluska, Haywood County; and the Baptists and Presbyterians, Ridgecrest and Montreat, Buncombe County. These resorts are descendants of the antebellum campgrounds and the assembly grounds first developed in the North such as Ocean Grove, New Jersey, and Lake Chautauqua, New York.

months, and it was immense and lavish. Huge boulders quarried from nearby mountains were brought down by train and slid into place "just as they are," moss and lichens untouched. Some weighed five tons. In the hotel's Great Hall, 120 feet long and 80 feet wide, stood two herculean fireplaces. Built with 120 tons of boulders and provided with andirons of half a ton each, they burned a small forest of 12-foot logs each year to keep patrons warm. Constructed on the side of Sunset Mountain, the inn overlooked the valley and the city and had a 100-acre golf course as a front lawn.

Like Grove himself, much of the inn's clientele flourished on newly won wealth. Most of the nation's older gentry had already chosen their favorite resorts: the Berkshires, Bar Harbor, Nahant. There they and their families fled the urban melting pot, its discomfort and diversity, for the rustic simplicity of unspoiled villages, quaint natives, and the comforts of caste affinity. Many who came to the Grove Park Inn were more like Grove—individuals whose inventiveness and talent had taken them to the top in a single lifetime. Thomas Edison, Henry Ford, Harry Firestone, Herbert Hoover, and Woodrow Wilson were among the inn's most prominent guests. The inn was an equally popular resort for guests from southern metropolises, the wealthiest of whom fled the summer's heat for months at a time. From Atlanta and Charleston, from New Orleans and Birmingham, they sent their saddle horses by train, brought their own maids and chauffeurs, shipped their automobiles by railroad, and moved in.

Daytime was for sport and socializing. At billiards and bowling, golf and tennis, hiking or bridge, the "best people" appreciated good fun and each other, leaving cares and less congenial social classes behind. Evenings were more regimented occasions. Indeed, the solemn formality of the inn's regulations suggests that Grove harbored some doubt that all his patrons would mind their manners spontaneously. A 1914 advertisement for the inn warned that the resort was "minus the bizarre, the tawdry, the flashily foolish." Dinner garb was white ties for men and evening dresses for ladies. (The sevencourse dinner took two hours to eat.) Men might smoke after dinner but ladies could not, except in the solitude of their own parlors. A good night's sleep was supremely important to Grove, as he made clear in an inn brochure: "A few people who prefer to retire late will thoughtlessly disturb hundreds who desire rest, by loud talking, slamming of doors, throwing shoes on the floor, and a dozen other annoyances. . . . We have the courage to enforce a discipline that makes rest possible." Three decisive steps maximized nocturnal repose at the Grove Inn. The flushing system for the toilets was turned off at 10:30 P.M. The gates to the driveway were closed at the same hour. And there was "not a double bed in the inn."

Biltmore House, Asheville, Buncombe County, 1895–1900. Courtesy Biltmore House and Gardens. The landscaping had only just begun as the tiny trees show.

A Mountain Refuge

By far the richest man attracted to the mountains of western North Carolina was George Vanderbilt. Son and grandson of railroad tycoons from New York, the bookish but shrewd twenty-six-year-old bachelor found the air and climate of Asheville invigorating and the scenery enchanting. In 1888 he purchased two thousand acres of land with the notion of building a summer house upon it for himself and his mother. Fortunately, the young millionaire's ideas about what to do with his estate were only half-formed, and he called upon an old family friend to advise him.

Black Forest Lodge, interior and exterior, Cradle of Forestry, Pisgah National Forest. This structure imitated the architecture Schenck knew in the Black Forest of his homeland.

The involvement of Frederick Law Olmsted in the shaping of what would become the Biltmore Estate and surrounding forests was momentous, for Olmsted was the designer of Central Park in New York and the nation's leading landscape architect. Olmsted immediately encouraged Vanderbilt to go beyond his initial thought of creating a manor and a private deer park: "The soil is poor, the woods are miserable. It's no place for a park." Olmsted urged Vanderbilt instead to embrace a purpose that was far more ambitious. He should transform the woods he had purchased—runts, ruins, and saplings, depleted by rapacious lumbering, ravaged by the practice of burning or girdling trees to clear land for pasturage—into a scenic and profitable forest. The key to success was the scientific management of the land and the trees on it. Vanderbilt had the unique opportunity to demonstrate to the nation the value of scientific forestry and to profit from it.

The multimillionaire built both his manor and a model estate. Designed by the aristocratic architect Richard M. Hunt of New York, Biltmore House was a country home without parallel in America. The monumental French chateau was built of Indiana limestone, hauled 600 miles to North Carolina and transported 3 miles from the main line to the house site on a $77,000 private railway spur. With the terrace and stables, the audacious mansion was 1,000 feet in length and encompassed 250 rooms, all furnished with art treasures from around the world. Its setting was superb and the view from it breathtaking. A critic had only one question: What was it doing "among the one-room cabins of Appalachian mountaineers?"

Yet, following Olmsted's counsel, Vanderbilt expanded his estate beyond a grandiose retreat in the wilderness. He bought over a hundred thousand more acres by the turn of the century, including the pinnacle peak of western North Carolina, Mount Pisgah. He built a model village for the employees of the estate, constructed road, water and drainage systems, and erected a schoolhouse and a hospital—in a countryside not accustomed to such amenities. For better and worse, Biltmore employees "were subjected to almost military discipline—compelled to be prompt, methodical, and continuous" in their labors.

The most enduring legacy of the Biltmore estate came in the domain of forest conservation. At Olmsted's suggestion, Vanderbilt hired Gifford Pinchot—a young Yale graduate and the first American to choose forestry as a profession—to manage his lands. He gave Pinchot the opportunity to demonstrate his belief that controlled timber cutting and reforestation, done in cooperation with enlightened commercial lumber companies, was the best way to conserve American forests from ignorant plunder. When Pinchot left—eventually to become the first forester in the United States Department of Agriculture—Vanderbilt placed Carl Schenck of Germany in charge of his lands. In 1898 Schenck founded the Biltmore Forest School, the first in America, and used the Vanderbilt forest for a campus. The historic role of Schenck and his three hundred young trainees on behalf of national conservation was acknowledged in 1961 with the designation of his school and its buildings as the "Cradle of Forestry" in America. Visitors can take the "campus tour," view exhibits, and walk trails that splendidly illustrate the history of that pioneering enterprise.

The joint creation of Vanderbilt and Olmsted, the millionaire and the landscape planner, became the property of the nation after Vanderbilt's death in 1914. For a modest sum, his widow sold almost a hundred thousand acres of the Biltmore estate to the National Forest Reservation Commission, specifying that it become a national preserve. The reforested domain of a single aristocrat became the recreational refuge of millions in 1917 and forms the bulk of North Carolina's modern Pisgah National Forest.

Ranger's dwelling, Cradle of Forestry, Pisgah National Forest. The first forestry school in America was an outgrowth of Dr. Carl Schenck's conservation and forestry management work for George Vanderbilt at Biltmore. From 1898 to 1913, when he abandoned it, the school attempted to teach practical forestry to the "sons of every lumberman and of every lumber owner in the country." In an age of awakening conservation movements to curb the ruthless exploitation of natural resources, Schenck's efforts eventually suffered from competition by the many institutions that started up forestry courses and degree programs of their own. Some of his buildings and a sense of his philosophy and work can be found at the Cradle of Forestry historic site.

The Price of Progress

North Carolina's participation in the world of industry and urbanization, commercial agriculture and tourism, began slowly in the 1870s, grew steadily through 1900, and exploded in the first two decades of the twentieth century. By the 1920s the state took pride in its reputation as the South's most progressive state—a land of factories and business enterprise as well as of farms, of good roads and improving schools, of urban vitality and civic achievement. In urban centers especially, an exuberant vision of progress had triumphed. Town tried to outpromote town and the state to outdo other states in heralding North Carolina and her communities as magnets of growth and commerce. In 1870 most North Carolinians relied on the skills of self-sufficiency to "make do." By 1920 thousands of Tar Heels were making money and thousands more aspired, with a little luck and capital and business cunning, to join the ranks of those who were getting ahead.

Most North Carolinians, like most Americans of the early twentieth century, celebrated the "go-ahead" spirit and driving economic ambition of the new era. When eight-story skyscrapers went up, they cheered and vied for space. When tourists flooded in, they expanded their businesses. When real estate values soared, they bought and sold. Every new automobile and macadamized street, every new power plant and telephone brought the Tar Heel state and its people further out of historic isolation and poverty and closer to the mainstream of national prosperity.

The physical world that North Carolinians saw around them by 1920 ranged from log cabins, flimsy shanties, and false storefronts to skyscrapers and the elegance of the latest churches. Architects were largely responsible for the expensive end of this gamut, and in North Carolina Frank P. Milburn's hand is seen everywhere. The courthouse with the top-story jail was his innovation. He built the Buncombe, Durham, Forsyth (demolished), Mecklenburg, and Vance county courthouses, as well as a host of railroad stations, college buildings, and banks.

The Lost Home of Thomas Wolfe

Yet not all Americans joined in praise of the new era, and not all North Carolinians applauded the triumph of a New South. Thomas Wolfe, born in Asheville in 1900 and reared in the community as it crossed the threshold from mountain hamlet to resort boom town, saw in the ambition unleashed by growth peril as well as profit, loss as well as liberation.

Emblem of the loss of "beauty and spirit" that Wolfe found at the core of the New South triumphant was the boardinghouse that his mother bought in 1906 and that she named "Old Kentucky Home." On the surface, the house with the nostalgic name strikes the visitor as a rambling turn-of-the-century home built on a large scale. A wide

(Opposite) Thomas Wolfe and his mother on the steps of "Old Kentucky Home," 1937. N.C. State Archives.

"Old Kentucky Home," Thomas Wolfe Memorial, Asheville, Buncombe County.

"It was situated five minutes from the public square, on a pleasant sloping middleclass street of small homes and boarding houses. Dixieland was a big cheaply constructed frame house of eighteen or twenty drafty high-ceilinged rooms: it had a rambling, unplanned, gabular appearance, and was painted a dirty yellow. It had a pleasant green front yard, not deep but wide, bordered by a row of young deep-bodied maples: there was a sloping depth of one hundred and ninety feet, a frontage of one hundred and twenty. And Eliza, looking toward the town, said: 'They'll put a street behind there some day.'

"In winter, the wind blew howling blasts under the skirts of Dixieland: its back end was built high off the ground on wet columns of rotting brick. Its big rooms were heated by a small furnace which sent up, when charged with fire, a hot dry enervation to the rooms of the first floor, and a gaseous but chill radiation to those upstairs." *Look Homeward, Angel.*

porch and scattered balconies, high-ceilinged rooms and a sizable kitchen, made the house fit either for a large Victorian family or for a small company of boarders. The piano and overstuffed chairs that crowded the living room suggest the possibility of music and warmth, while the spare furnishings of the bedrooms present a contrast of cold austerity.

There was no ambivalence about the boardinghouse in the memory of Thomas Wolfe. "Old Kentucky Home" stood for the disruption of his family. Julia Wolfe, mother of eight children who lived past infancy, bought the dwelling at the age of forty-five. In towns with high numbers of tourists or new residents, many married or widowed middle-class women found security and a respectable career in the operation of boardinghouses. Julia Wolfe left the family home to oversee her business venture and took her seven-year-old son, Tom, to live with her. Her husband, W. O. Wolfe, remained home with the older children, a few hundred yards away. From that point on the youngest son—"with two roofs and no home"—felt that he was a vagabond and a stranger and burned inwardly with the need to understand his loss.

When Thomas Wolfe emerged as a writer in late adolescence, his divided family and the boardinghouse became the focus of his fiction, and both came to stand for the darker possibilities of "Progress" in the South and the nation. In two highly autobiographical novels, *Look Homeward, Angel* and *Of Time and the River,* and in dozens of short stories, Wolfe chronicled the turbulent epic of a family and a region divided and transformed by "money-hunger." The father's sense of tragedy and the vicissitudes of life bred in him a fatalistic "terror and hatred of property." It was "a curse and a care, and the tax collector gets all you have in the end." But, for the mother and for thousands of others in the New South, "property and freedom" were one and the same. The "mounting lust for ownership" that characterized the mother and the era inevitably became a mania for acquisition and brought not comfort but chaos in its wake. As if to leave no doubt that he saw the boardinghouse as a symbol of the South, Thomas Wolfe gave it the fictional name of "Dixieland."

The "mountainous verbal splendor" of Wolfe's prose and his lyrical portrait of "life, life, life" where he grew up—"savage, cruel, kind, noble, passionate, selfish, generous, stupid, ugly, beautiful, painful, joyous"—established him as one of the great American novelists of the century. Few writers ever matched Wolfe in his evocation of small-town society in the first decades of the twentieth century. Wolfe brought vibrantly to life the candy shop with its luscious temptations and the drugstore limeade so cold it made the head ache, the Jewish grocery with its sour pickles, the saloon, and the bawdy house. His fiction abounded with all the extraordinary characters who gave the community its magic and its mystery.

Mr. Wolfe's bedroom.

But the "naked intensity" of the young author made him enemies at home. He did not disguise his raw scorn for "Cheap Boosters" who believed that "we are . . . four times as civilized as our grandfathers because we go four times as fast in automobiles, because our buildings are four times as tall." He did not retreat from a rebellious determination to "say what I think of those people" who "shout 'Progress, Progress, Progress.'" The response to Wolfe's work by some in his native state was bitterness. Wrote one editor: "North Carolina and the South are spat upon."

Wolfe found his family more sympathetic to his claim that his book was "not written about people in Asheville—it is written about people everywhere." Their understanding of the family's "young Shakespeare" was fortunate, for it was through the passionately candid story of strife in a family strikingly like his own—the father a volatile stonecutter, the woman a wife who left her husband's home to open a boardinghouse—that Wolfe explored the consequences of the fevered pursuit of property and profit.

"Eliza saw Altamont not as so many hills, buildings, people: she saw it in the pattern of a gigantic blueprint. She knew the history of every piece of valuable property—who bought it, who sold it, who owned it in 1893, and what it was now worth. She was sensitive to every growing-pain of the young town, gauging from year to year its growth in any direction, and deducing the probable direction of its future expansion. 'There'll be a street through here some day.'" *Look Homeward, Angel.*

Wolfe contrasted life in the boardinghouse and his existence there against the turbulent vitality of the nearby home he grew up in. To the novelist, the two dwellings symbolized the gulf between the "guarded and sufficient strength" of the Victorian household and the unstable and rootless modern world. The home of his first six years no longer stands, but the writer recalled it as a solid and spacious house, designed like many middle-class dwellings to be a bastion of family privacy and a retreat from the stress of work and commerce. Life within the household was both warm and explosive. At the center was a father who was an extraordinary Victorian individualist. Theatrical and lavish, given to comic tirades and periodic alcoholic binges, he was the very opposite of his prudent and parsimonious wife. The family "came to look forward eagerly to his entrance" after a day's work, "for he brought with him the great gusto of living, of ritual. They would watch him in the evening as he turned the corner

The bathroom down the hall.

below with eager strides, follow carefully the processional of his movements from the time he flung his provisions upon the kitchen table to the re-kindling of his fire, with which he was always at odds when he entered, and onto which he poured wood, coal and kerosene lavishly."

It was no wonder that the move with his mother to the boardinghouse left the boy vanquished, certain that he had "lost forever the . . . warm centre of his home." Gone was privacy, for in the boardinghouse he had to share food and shelter with strangers. Gone was space and bounty. "As the house filled, they went from room to little room, going successively down the shabby scale of their lives." There was no bed, not even a "quilt to call our own that might not be taken from us to warm the mob that rocks upon the porch and grumbles." Gone even was physical warmth. To save money, the mother scrimped on coal in the winter, walked around the house in an old sweater and a castoff man's coat, and left "Dixieland" a "chill tomb."

Had Wolfe chosen his family as a subject of a history rather than as the springboard of his fiction, he might have produced a far different interpretation of his parents' struggles. The history might have placed his parents' turmoil and his mother's boardinghouse at the very center of crosscurrents of change in family life that were beginning to emerge in North Carolina and the nation by the turn of the century. The son might have questioned why his mother married W. O. Wolfe in 1880. He was a dashing man with a business and a house of his own, to be sure; but he was nonetheless a man she hardly knew. Thomas Wolfe might have answered that for any young woman of twenty-five in 1880—even one like Julia, independent enough to have gone to college, taught school, sold books, and purchased real estate—independence without marriage was no virtue. "Marriage—even to a gatepost—was the only estate to which a woman should aspire."

But, twenty-five years after her marriage, Julia Wolfe certainly knew that new ideas about the independence of women were emerging. A quasi-separation from her family and entry into business would no longer make her an outcast. Many other women were, directly or indirectly, "getting out of the house," transforming themselves and society in the process. Some from the middle and upper classes joined the Women's Christian Temperance Union and sought through the WCTU to end the reign of the saloons that so undermined family tranquillity. (Before her marriage, Julia Westall Wolfe was an active temperance reformer.) Other women were joining women's clubs —North Carolina's first was founded in Charlotte in 1902—which sought first the physical beautification and then the moral uplift of their communities. Still others joined the Social Purity Movement, which fought to close down brothels, rehabilitate prostitutes, and

"He built his house close to the quiet hilly street; he bedded the loamy soil with flowers; he laid the short walk to the high veranda steps with great square sheets of colored marble; he put a fence of spiked iron between his house and the world." *Look Homeward, Angel.*

Kitchen of "Old Kentucky Home."

The traditional view of women that the woman's movement has had to combat was shared even by other women, such as Helen Campbell in her *Household Economics*, 1896: "Cleaning can never pass from Women's hands . . . for to keep the world clean, this is the one great task for woman."

99

Carrie Nation in the early 1900s. N.C. State Archives. Six feet tall, fearless, and a drunkard's wife, she attacked saloons with word and hatchet and helped create a mood favorable to the national prohibition of alcoholic drink.

The difference women could make in public affairs was noted: "The improvement of health, the betterment of morals, the modernizing of education and the humanizing of penology are perhaps the most vital matters of government in which North Carolina women have interested themselves. Any one who can deny either that all these things need improvement or that the activity of the Federated [Women's] Clubs has improved them betrays a startling ignorance of the facts in this state." *The Southerner*, 28 January 1912.

convert men from the sexual double standard to a more civilized code of self-control and abstinence.

Julia Wolfe left her home at a time of intensified public debate over "woman's place." With urgency and unprecedented forthrightness, social critics were asking whether it was woman's sole task to provide "touches of beauty and oases of calm for men harried by their work, ambition, and insecurity." Was it woman's highest fulfilment to rear a family and sacrifice her own needs to those of others? There were abundant indications that women were becoming an "unquiet sex": the widely noted restlessness of women confined to the home, the 100 percent rise in divorces from 1900 to 1920, the rush of young women to colleges and the refusal of many to settle down with husband and family, the small but increasing number of women who were seeking work or careers. With magazines publicly challenging the family household as a "prison and a burden and a tyrant," with feminists calling on women not only to demand the right to vote but to take up paying work outside the home, it was no surprise that one writer called the seething feminine discontent a "volcano."

But almost certainly Thomas Wolfe would have rejected women's restlessness as the reason for the family break and his mother's boardinghouse. He would have insisted on the centrality of his own vision: that the turbulence in his family's life, and of the life of the community and region around him, was connected with the disruptive triumph of the "New South." Everywhere that "Progress" prevailed it brought new wealth, but everywhere it also exacted a price. Beauty became ugliness; commerce triumphed over humanity. Asheville had once been a small mountain town, Wolfe's "centre of the earth." Flashy enough for young men to stride downtown wearing peg-top yellow shoes, flaring striped trousers, and broad-brimmed hats with colored bands, the town before its conquest by an ethos of progress was nonetheless a place where "Life buzzed slowly like a fly." Even the "thick plume of the fountain" near city hall rose "in slow pulses," fell upon itself, and slapped the pool in lazy rhythms. In Wolfe's vision, Asheville's "beauty and spirit" were lost when the city capitulated to tourists, the real estate boom, and "cheap Board of Trade boosters."

In the mountain countryside, the pattern was the same: economic profit, spiritual loss, beauty disfigured. Slopes and forests "had been ruinously detimbered; the farm soil on hill sides had eroded and washed down"; deserted mines scarred the landscape. "It was evident that a huge compulsive greed had been at work: the region had been sucked and gutted, milked dry, denuded of its rich primeval treasures: something blind and ruthless had been here, grasped, and gone." The New South had lured away the young of the countryside, swept them off to the town, leaving behind kinfolk "withdrawn from the world." Those who stayed remained in the great Blue Ridge for their love of its immense wild grandeur and rocky streams, holding on to their patch of earth. But, in Wolfe's view, "their inheritance was bare."

Of progress and its perils in his region, of the richness and rending of his family, and later of his tempestuous life in the North, Thomas Wolfe was to write more than a million words. As he traveled beyond the South, he observed everywhere what he had first seen in North Carolina and the boardinghouse of his youth: an obsession with money, an equation of life with the latest goods and styles. Unable to celebrate the triumph of a consumer society in his native state or the nation, Wolfe worried that "we are lost here in America." "We've become like a nation of advertising men, all hiding behind catch phrases like 'prosperity' and 'rugged individualism' and 'the American way.' And the real things like freedom, and equal opportunity, and the integrity and worth of the individual—things that belonged to the American dream since the beginning—they have become just words too." Yet ultimately the novelist from Asheville was not despondent. The "true fulfillment of our spirit, of our people, of our mighty and immortal land, is yet to come. I think that the true discovery of our own democracy is still before us." For Thomas Wolfe and for other North Carolinians, the American dream was yet to be accomplished, but its achievement was as "certain as the morning, as inevitable as noon." Whether Wolfe the critic or Wolfe the optimist was correct, the decades ahead would determine.

Acknowledgments

The efforts of many persons have gone into this work. The suggestions that resulted from our public appeal for information as well as the knowledge of experts in many areas have enhanced the quality of this book and facilitated its production. Volunteers who led us to privately owned sites and out-of-the-way places have added materially to the gathering and scope of the information in this volume. To all these contributors the staff is sincerely grateful. We especially wish to thank Peggy Boswell, Charlotte Brown, Mary Canada, Bessie Carrington, William Chafe, Guy Coe, Jerry Cotten, Betty Cowan, Thelma Dempsey, James Dorman, R. Neil Fulghum, Raymond Gavins, Philip Guy, Grace Guyer, Jacquelyn Hall, H. G. Jones, Robert Kenzer, Jo White Linn, John A. McNeill, Sr., Frances Moody, Malvin E. Moore, Dan L. Morrill, Pauline Myrick, Allan Paul, William Reddy, Jane Rowe, Peyton Russ, Dorothy Sapp, Judith Smith, George Stevenson, Jr., Elizabeth Turner, W. Kirby Watson, Peter Wood, Anne Wortham, and Betty O. Young.

The staffs of various institutions have also aided our research: the Manuscript Department of the William R. Perkins Library and the East Campus Library, Duke University; the North Carolina Collection and the Southern Historical Collection of the Louis R. Wilson Library, University of North Carolina at Chapel Hill; the University Archives of the D. H. Hill Library, North Carolina State University; and the Historical Publications, Technical Services, Iconographic Records, Survey and Planning, Archives and Records, and Historic Sites areas of the Division of Archives and History, North Carolina Department of Cultural Resources. To all of them it is a pleasure to acknowledge our indebtedness and thanks.

(Opposite) Child under the hop vine. Photograph by Margaret Morley. N.C. State Archives.

Bibliography

Printed Sources

Ashe, Samuel A., ed. *Biographical History of North Carolina from Colonial Times to the Present*. 8 vols. Greensboro, 1905.

Baltzell, E. Digby. *The Protestant Establishment: Aristocracy and Caste in America*. New York, 1964.

Banks, Ann, ed. *First-Person America*. New York, 1980.

Bluestone, Dan. "The Southern Railway Company." Report, Heritage Conservation and Recreation Service, 1977.

Bobinski, George S. *Carnegie Libraries: Their History and Impact on American Public Library Development*. Chicago, 1969.

Brawley, James S. *Rowan County: A Brief History*. Raleigh, 1974.

Campbell, Helen S. *Household Economics*. New York, ca. 1896.

Cash, W. J. *The Mind of the South*. New York, 1941.

Champion, Myra. *The Lost World of Thomas Wolfe*. Asheville, 1970.

The City of Raleigh, N.C., and Vicinity: Conditions and Resources. Raleigh, n. d.

The City of Raleigh. Raleigh, 1887.

Clark, Thomas D. *Pills, Petticoats and Plows: The Southern Country Store, 1865–1914*. Indianapolis and New York, 1944.

Crum, Mason. *The Story of Lake Junaluska*. Greensboro, 1950.

Dixon, Roger. *Victorian Architecture*. New York, 1978.

Dowd, Jerome. "Strikes and Lockouts in North Carolina." *Gunton's Magazine*, February 1901.

Durden, Robert F. *The Dukes of Durham, 1865–1929*. Durham, 1975.

Edmonds, Helen G. *The Negro and Fusion Politics in North Carolina, 1896–1901*. Chapel Hill, 1951.

Edwards, Richard. *Contested Terrain: The Transformation of the Work Place in the Twentieth Century*. New York, 1979.

Escott, Paul. *Slavery Remembered: A Record of Twentieth-Century Slave Narratives*. Chapel Hill, 1979.

Fein, Albert. *Frederick Law Olmsted and the American Environmental Tradition*. New York, 1972.

Funk, Linda. *The Duke Homestead Guidebook*. Raleigh, 1978.

Gavins, Raymond. "Black Leadership in North Carolina to 1900." In *The Black Presence in North Carolina*, edited by Rodney Barfield and Jeffrey Crow. Raleigh, 1978.

Giedion, Sigfried. *Mechanization Takes Command*. New York, 1948.

Ginns, Patsy Moore. *Rough Weather Makes Good Timber*. Chapel Hill, 1977.

Girouard, Mark. *Sweetness and Light: The Queen Anne Movement, 1860–1900*. Oxford, Eng., 1977.

Glass, Brent. "Southern Mill Hills: Design in a 'Public' Place." In *Carolina Dwelling*, edited by Doug Swaim. Raleigh, 1978.

Goodwyn, Lawrence. *Democratic Promise: The Populist Moment in America*. New York, 1976.

Hayden, Harry. *The Wilmington Rebellion*. N.p., 1936.

"Healthful Habits at the Grove Park Inn." *Southern Living*, October 1977.

Hobbs, Peter Burke. "Plantation to Factory: Tradition and Industrialization in Durham, N.C., 1880–1900." Master's thesis, Duke University, 1971.

Holt, Lanier Rand. "'I Had to Like It': A Study of a Durham Textile Community." Honors essay, University of North Carolina at Chapel Hill, 1977.

Hughes, Julian. *Development of the Textile Industry in Alamance County*. Burlington, N.C., 1965.

Janiewski, Dolores. "From Field to Factory: Race, Class, Sex, and the Woman Worker in Durham, 1880–1940." Ph.D. dissertation, Duke University, 1979.

Jolley, Harley E. "The Cradle of Forestry in America." Reprint from *American Forests* 76, nos. 10–12 (Oct.–Dec., 1970).

Johnson, Mary Elizabeth, ed. *Times Down Home: 75 Years With the 'Progressive Farmer.'* Birmingham, Ala., 1978.

Kelly, Fred, ed. *Miracle at Kitty Hawk: The Letters of Wilbur and Orville Wright*. New York, 1951.

Kraft, Stephanie. *No Castles on Main Street: American Authors and Their Homes*. Chicago, 1979.

Kuhn, Clifford. "Industrialization in Burlington." Report, Southern Oral History Program, 1978.

Lefler, Hugh T., and Newsome, Albert R. *North Carolina: The History of a Southern State*. 3d ed. Chapel Hill, 1973.

Lincoln, C. Eric. "Black Religion in North Carolina, from Colonial Times to 1900." In *The Black Presence in North Carolina*, edited by Rodney Barfield and Jeffrey Crow. Raleigh, 1978.

(Opposite) Well at Glencoe.

Little-Stokes, Ruth. "Dilworth Historic District." Report, N.C. Division of Archives and History, 1978.

Litwack, Leon. *Been in the Storm So Long: The Aftermath of Slavery.* New York, 1979.

Maass, John. *The Victorian Home in America.* New York, 1972.

McDaniel, George. *Hearth and Home: Preserving a People's Culture.* Philadelphia, 1981.

McDuffie, Jerome A. "Politics in Wilmington and New Hanover County, North Carolina, 1865–1900: The Genesis of a Race Riot." Ph.D. dissertation, Kent State University, 1979.

McMath, Robert C. "Agrarian Protest at the Forks of the Creek." *North Carolina Historical Review* 51 (Winter 1974): 41–63.

Martin, Vickie. "Biography of Pearl De-Zern Martin." Paper, Duke University, 1980.

Morehouse, H. L. *H. M. Tupper, D. D.: A Narrative of Twenty-Five Years' Work in the South.* New York, 1890.

Morrill, Dan L. "Dilworth: Charlotte's Initial Streetcar Suburb." Paper, in the possession of the author, n. d.

Murphy, Mary. "Burlington." Report, Southern Oral History Program, 1980.

Murray, Pauli. *Proud Shoes: The Story of an American Family.* New York, 1956.

Newman, Dale. "Work and Community Life in a Southern Textile Town." *Labor History* 19 (Spring 1978): 204–25.

Noblin, Stuart. *Leonidas LaFayette Polk, Agrarian Crusader.* Chapel Hill, 1949.

Parker, Inez Moore. *The Biddle-Johnson C. Smith University Story.* Charlotte, 1975.

Perkins, Elsie Wallace. "Reminiscences of a Durham Childhood: The Turn of the Century." In *Durham: A Pictorial History*, edited by Joel A. and Frank A. Kostyu. Norfolk, 1978.

Pierpont, Andrew Warren. "Development of the Textile Industry in Alamance County." Ph.D. dissertation, University of North Carolina at Chapel Hill, 1953.

Pinehurst, North Carolina. Boston, 1908.

Prince, Richard E. *Southern Railway System Steam Locomotives and Boats.* Green River, Wyo., 1970.

Ransom, Robert L., and Sutch, Richard. *One Kind of Freedom: The Economic Consequences of Emancipation.* Cambridge, 1977.

Robbins, Tyler B. "The Work Experience: The Durham Hosiery Mill, 1898–1976." Unpublished paper, Duke University, 1978.

Robinson, Blackwell P., ed. *The North Carolina Guide.* Chapel Hill, 1955.

Rodgers, Daniel T. "Tradition, Modernity, and the American Industrial Worker." *Journal of Interdisciplinary History* 7 (Spring 1977): 655–81.

————. *The Work Ethic in Industrial America, 1850–1920.* Chicago, 1978.

Roper, Laura Wood. *FLO: A Biography of Frederick Law Olmsted.* Baltimore, 1973.

Russ, Peyton F. "A Design History of Reynolda Gardens, 1910–1920." Report, Reynolda House, 1977.

St. Joseph's A.M.E. Church Directory, 1969. N.p. 1969.

Scott, Anne. *The Southern Lady: From Pedestal to Politics, 1830–1930.* Chicago, 1970.

Shackelford, Laurel, and Weinberg, Bill, eds. *Our Appalachia: An Oral History.* New York, 1977.

Spencer, Alonzo T., Jr. "The Making of Reynolda House: Learning Center and Museum of American Art." Master's thesis, Wake Forest University, 1978.

Taylor, A. Elizabeth. "The Woman Suffrage Movement in North Carolina." *North Carolina Historical Review* 38 (1961): 45–62, 173–89.

Taylor, Rosser H. *Carolina Crossroads*. Murfreesboro, N.C., 1966.

Terrill, Tom, and Hirsch, Jerrold, eds. *Such as Us: Southern Voices of the Thirties*. Chapel Hill, 1978.

Tilley, Nannie May. *The Bright-Tobacco Industry, 1860–1929*. Chapel Hill, 1948.

Tindall, George Brown. *The Emergence of the New South, 1913–1945*. Baton Rouge, 1967.

Tompkins, Daniel A. *History of Mecklenburg County and the City of Charlotte*. 2 vols. Charlotte, 1903.

Turnbull, Andrew. *Thomas Wolfe*. New York, 1967.

Van Noppen, Ina W. and John J. *Western North Carolina Since the Civil War*. Boone, N.C., 1973.

Walls, William J. *The African Methodist Episcopal Zion Church: Reality of the Black Church*. Charlotte, 1974.

Weare, Walter B. *Black Business in the New South: A Social History of the North Carolina Mutual Life Insurance Company*. Urbana, Ill., 1973.

Wiebe, Robert H. *The Search for Order, 1877–1920*. New York, 1967.

Williams, Alexa C. *Raleigh: A Guide to North Carolina's Capital*. Raleigh, 1975.

Wilson, Emily Herring. *George Henry Black, 100 Years*. Winston-Salem, 1979.

Wilson, Peter M. *Southern Exposure*. Chapel Hill, 1927.

Wolfe, Thomas. *Look Homeward, Angel*. New York, 1929.

Woodward, C. Vann. *Origins of the New South, 1877–1913*. Baton Rouge, 1951.

Zimmermann, Hilda Jane. "Penal Reform Movement in the South during the Progressive Era, 1890–1917." *Journal of Southern History* 17 (November 1951): 462–92.

Newspapers

Alamance *Gleaner*, October and November 1900.

Durham *Tobacco Plant*, 22 February 1882, 8 December 1886.

Greensboro *Daily News* (special edition), 29 May 1971.

Raleigh *News and Observer*, 5 April 1896.

Manuscript Sources

Manuscript Department, William R. Perkins Library, Duke University, Durham.

W. Duke Sons & Co. Papers.

Charles N. Hunter Papers.

Stowe Family Papers, Account Book, 1856–1874.

Tillinghast Family Papers.

James King Wilkerson Papers, 1898 Almanac.

Southern Historical Collection, Louis R. Wilson Library, University of North Carolina, Chapel Hill.

Thomas Settle Papers.

Interviews

Students affiliated with the Southern Oral History Program (SOHP) at the University of North Carolina at Chapel Hill and the Oral History Program (OHP) at Duke University have recovered remarkable materials on North Carolina since 1900 through interviews with men and women whose memories range back to the early twentieth century. Of the interviews used for this volume, the following were of special value:

Bessie Buchanan, interviewed by Lanier Rand. SOHP.

Luther Ellis Burch, interviewed by Daniel Ellison. SOHP.

Thomas Burt, interviewed by Glen Hinson. SOHP.

George Carroll, interviewed by Tyler B. Robbins. OHP.

I. L. Dean, interviewed by Richard C. Franck. OHP.

Pearl DeZern Martin, interviewed by Vickie W. Martin. OHP.

James Dorman, interviewed by Sydney Nathans. OHP.

Paul Faucette, interviewed by Allen Tullos. SOHP.

Ethel Faucette, interviewed by Allen Tullos. SOHP.

Fred Greenhill, interviewed by Tyler B. Robbins. OHP.

John Maynard Jones, interviewed by Dolores Janiewski. OHP.

Ethel Lovell, interviewed by Julia L. Frey. OHP.

Reginald Mitchener, interviewed by Glen Hinson. SOHP.

Charles Murray, interviewed by Brent Glass. SOHP.

Zelma Montgomery Murray, interviewed by Brent Glass. SOHP.

Janie Cameron Riley, interviewed by George McDaniel. OHP.

Daisy J. Weadon, interviewed by Mark Weadon. OHP.

In addition to these university collections, two independent interviews have also been used:

Elizabeth Williams of Charlotte, interviewed by Elizabeth Turner.

Interview of Fred Loring Seely, Jr. In *Our Appalachia: An Oral History*, edited by Laurel Shackelford and Bill Weinberg. New York, 1977.

1 Clay County
Courthouse, *Hayesville*.

Swain County
Mingus Mill, Pioneer Farmstead, *U.S. #441, Great Smoky Mountains National Park*.
Pioneer Farmstead, *U.S. #441, Great Smoky Mountains National Park*.

Haywood County
Lake Junaluska.

Transylvania County
Cradle of Forestry, *Mount Pisgah National Forest*.

Buncombe County
Biltmore House and Gardens, *Asheville*.
Courthouse, *Asheville*.
Grove Park Inn, *Asheville*.
Montreat.
Ridgecrest.
Thomas Wolfe Memorial, *Asheville*.

Burke County
Henry River Mill Village, *off I-40 on S.R. #1803*.
Valdese.

Watauga County
Green Park Hotel, *Blowing Rock*.
Mast Store, *Valle Crucis*.

Ashe County
Grassy Creek Methodist Church.

Alleghany County
Piney Creek Primitive Baptist Church.

Catawba County
Propst House, *Shuford Memorial Gardens, Hickory*.

2 Mecklenburg County
Biddle Hall and Carnegie Library, *Johnson C. Smith University, Charlotte*.
Dilworth, *Charlotte*.
Latta Arcade, *Charlotte*.
Myers Park, *Charlotte*.
Old Courthouse, *Charlotte*.

Iredell County
Courthouse and Post Office (now Statesville City Hall).

Union County
Courthouse, *Monroe*.

Cabarrus County
Concord Depot.

Rowan County
File's General Store, *Bringle Ferry Road near Morgan*.
Livingstone College, *Salisbury*.
Rufty's General Store, *Salisbury*.
Spencer Shops.

Forsyth County
Körner's Folly, *Kernersville*.
Pepper's Warehouse, *Winston-Salem*.
Reynolda House and Gardens, *Winston-Salem*.

Stokes County
Jessup's Mill, *S.R. #1432 north of Francisco*.

Guilford County
Fordham's Drugstore, *Greensboro*.
Oakdale Cotton Mills, *Jamestown*.

Davidson County
Thomasville Depot.

Randolph County
Coleridge Mill Village.
St. Paul's Methodist Church (now North Randolph Historical Society Museum), *Randleman*.

Richmond County
Hamlet Depot.

Moore County
Bellview Schoolhouse, *Moore County Board of Education grounds, U.S. #1 south of Sanford*.
Pinehurst.

Chatham County
Lystra Baptist Church, *Lystra Church Road, off U.S. #15-501*.

Alamance County
Glencoe Mill Village, *off N.C. #62*.

Caswell County
Hamer General Store, *N.C. #62 northeast of Yanceyville*.

3 Durham County
Blackwell's Tobacco Factory (now American Tobacco Company), *201 W. Pettigrew St., Durham*.
Old Courthouse, *Durham*.
Duke Homestead, *Durham*.
Lacy's Store, *Bahama*.
Old N.C. Mutual and Provident Society (now Mechanics and Farmers Bank), *Parrish St., Durham*.
North Carolina Central University, *Durham*.
St. Joseph's A.M.E. Church (now St. Joseph's Historical Foundation), *804 Fayetteville St., Durham*.
Trinity Park, *Durham*.

Map of Historic Places

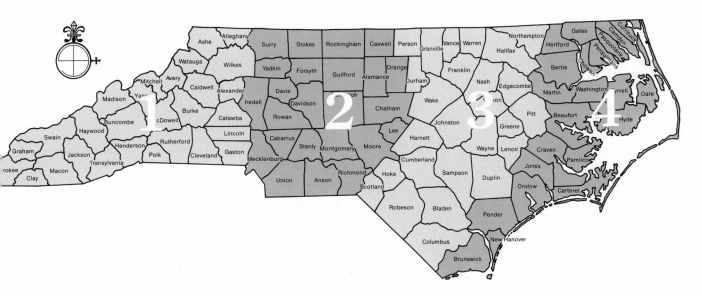

Wake County
Apex Town Hall.
Briggs's Hardware Store, *Fayetteville Street Mall, Raleigh.*
Estey Hall, *Shaw University, Raleigh.*
Executive Mansion, *Raleigh.*
Holladay Hall, *North Carolina State University, Raleigh.*
Oakwood, *Raleigh.*
Pullen Park and Carousel, *Western Blvd., Raleigh.*
St. Paul A.M.E. Zion Church, *Raleigh.*

Robeson County
Philadelphus Schoolhouse, *Robeson County Educational Resource Center, N.C. #72 northwest of Lumberton.*

Columbus County
Alliance Hall, *U.S. #701 north of Whiteville.*

Wayne County
Schoolhouse, *Governor Aycock's Birthplace.*

Franklin County
Laurel Mill, *S.R. #1432, Gupton vicinity.*

Nash County
Country Doctor Museum, *Bailey.*

Vance County
Courthouse, *Henderson.*
Zollicoffer's Law Office, *Main St., Henderson.*
Henderson Fire Station, *Main Street.*

Warren County
Chapel of the Good Shepherd, *Ridgeway vicinity.*

Edgecombe County
Fenner's Warehouse, *Rocky Mount.*
Historic District, *Tarboro.*
Princeville.
Tarboro Depot.

4 New Hanover
St. Stephen A.M.E. Church, *S. 7th St., Wilmington.*

Beaufort County
Swindell's Store, *Bath.*
Washington Depot.

Dare County
Wright Brothers National Memorial, *Kitty Hawk.*

Index